# ENOUGH

## "with" ENOUGH

### Letters of Encouragement

## FOR WOMEN STRUGGLING UNDER THE
## WEIGHT OF A CHRISTIAN LIFE

A CURATED COLLECTION OF ESSAYS FROM HIGHER THINGS

Published by:
1517 Publishing
PO Box 54032
Irvine, CA 92619-4032

---

Publisher's Cataloging-in-Publication
(Provided by Cassidy Cataloguing Services, Inc.)

Names: Higher Things (Organization), author.
Title: Enough with "Enough" : letters of encouragement for women struggling under the weight of a Christian life / Higher Things.
Description: Irvine, CA : 1517 Publishing, [2025] | Series: Letters of encouragement | Includes bibliographical references.
Identifiers: ISBN: 978-1-964419-34-3 (paperback) | 978-1-964419-35-0 (ebook)
Subjects: LCSH: Christian women—Religious life. | Christian life. | Self-esteem in women—Religious aspects—Christianity. | God (Christianity) | Sex role—Religious aspects—Christianity. | BISAC: RELIGION / Christianity / Lutheran. | RELIGION / Christian Living / Women's Interests.
Classification: LCC: BV4527 .H54 2025 | DDC: 248.8/43—dc23

---

Printed in the United States of America.

Cover art by Julie Meyer.

# ENOUGH
## *with*
## "ENOUGH"

## *Letters of Encouragement*
### FOR WOMEN STRUGGLING UNDER THE
### WEIGHT OF A CHRISTIAN LIFE

A CURATED COLLECTION OF ESSAYS FROM HIGHER THINGS

"To be honest, I was initially hesitant to read yet another "inspirational book for Christian women." Most books in this genre overflow with chapter after chapter of instructions on what to do and what not to do to be more faithful women, often relying on seemingly "feminine" thematic hooks like wine, crafts, chocolate, or even laundry. However, knowing Higher Things and its laser focus on proclaiming the Good News, I really hoped this would be something different. Little did I know just how unique and overwhelmingly Gospel-centered it would be!

Reading this book feels like sitting down over coffee with a dear friend—one you trust not to flinch at the sin-broken and sinful realities of your life. This friend sees you, loves you in the midst of your complicated struggles, and tenderly applies the soothing balm of the pure Gospel to console your troubled soul. Without resorting to feminist tropes, these authors encourage women in their faith, no matter the situations or stations they find themselves in. They avoid the vapid and clumsy approaches of other Christian books, that instruct women to "be better," "sin less," "pray more," or "just spend more time with God." You won't find those tired suggestions here.

Instead, readers are reminded—again and again, in every single chapter—of what Christ Jesus has already done for them on the Cross. That their many sins are fully forgiven in Him, and that they are free from the bondage of the Law. Women in today's world, our culture, and within the LCMS desperately need to hear these bold, unequivocal truths—completely free of caveats or conditions. You have reminded me why I am still Lutheran. Thank you, ladies, for daring to speak up and write for us! And thank you, Higher Things, for providing the platform to make this possible."

*Sandra (Ostapowich) Madden is the former Content Executive for Higher Things, Inc. Since retiring from HT, she has become a partner at Joseph E. Madden, CPA, and is an Enrolled Agent (EA) licensed by the IRS.*

"*Enough with "Enough"* is yet again a faithful Lutheran offering from Higher Things. The essay authors are women just like you. Living out everyday lives focused on Jesus; they offer sincere and practical reflections that hearten sisters in Christ. This book speaks to women of all ages and vocations. After reading it once you will want to return to it again and again to be reminded that Christ is for you, pouring out His love and forgiveness on you each and every day. Enough with Enough will be a blessing to all who read it."

*Deaconess Dr. Tiffany Manor, Managing Director*
*LCMS National Mission, St. Louis, MO*

# Table of Contents

# Forward (On Mentorship)

*Becky Clausen*

## WOMENTORING: Gospel, Identity, and Sisterhood in Christ

"Womentoring": women mentoring women. What comes to mind when you think about women mentoring women in the church? I picture a polished, organized, ducks-in-a-row kind of woman. She is never seen re-wearing an outfit; she whips up the most delicious potluck dishes, saying, "It was nothing," and you just know her life is sparkling clean. Wow, this ideal woman takes my breath away! Perfection may get more "likes" on social media, but if we are going to discuss the point of Christian mentorship, a spotless image is not our goal. All airbrushed imagery we might attach to other women (or ourselves), whether in church or in our daily lives, imprison us in unworthiness. The false laws we craft are lies that prevent us from loving God's revealed law, which is for our good and fulfilled for us by Christ. These lies act as brick walls to seeing Christ our Savior, block our path to the cross, scrape us up when we take refuge in them, and knock us out with a brick to the head when we trust in them for worthiness, purpose, and identity. Well, yikes!

The brick wall of lies must be destroyed! The lies whisper that we are only loved if we are perfect. The lies promise that we will finally be seen and heard once we have made ourselves lovable—just be pretty enough or smart enough or (fill in the bank). The lies' perpetual chorus is that we are only worthy and worthwhile once we have achieved an always-changing and never-attainable standard. Shake the red-brick dust off, and let's focus on the Truth. Perfect women instructing other women to be perfect is NOT our goal! It is imperfect women, forgiven women, REDEEMED women embracing each other and leading each other back to Christ, back to the cross, back to the font, back to where He has won our forgiveness and secured our salvation. Our strength is found in Christ Jesus who has already defeated all lies for us. Jesus lived a perfect life, died a bloody death to pay the sacrificial price for every sin, winning our complete forgiveness, and then He rose victorious—for us.

The finished work of Jesus gives us a new identity. This Gospel of Christ Jesus for us is the best news! The Gospel swings the door open for women to respond by leading each other back to where salvation was won. We stand before God, clothed in Christ Jesus. Forgiven is our new identity; we are washed clean, adopted through Baptism into God's family, gifted His holiness, and granted faith and eternal salvation because of what Jesus has done for us. We continually guide each other, particularly when we are tempted to struggle on our own, to the tomb where the stone is forever rolled away and is forever empty for us. Just as Jesus called forgiven Mary Magdalene by name in the garden on that first Easter morning, He calls us by name, too! God shows His love for us that while we were still sinners, Christ died for us (Romans 5:8). Christ's victory is ours! The greatest care we can take of each other as God's baptized daughters has us returning always to where salvation is won and He who won it.

Life can be dark, and there may be times on this journey when remembering our identity in Christ feels impossible to do alone. When we get stuck in darkness, it's easy to end up suffering silently or wearing the mask of "I'm fine." Here is where Satan preys on us. Whether we crawl into isolation and fear, dance with unworthiness, or in despair, convince ourselves we are unlovable, it's at these times a Christian sister can help us seek The Truth. How do we help? God promises to be present where His Word is preached and His sacraments are rightly administered, so inviting or sitting next to a friend in church is a blessing. Encouraging her to go to Confession and Absolution, praying for her, reading Scripture, and sharing the Good News all redirect us to the love of Christ. We have no perfect words or lives but a gracious and merciful God who loves us, who takes all sin into Himself, and who suffers a bloody, brutal death to pay for every speck of unbelief, fear, separation, isolation, despair, personal inadequacies, and all lies that we forge into brick walls. We are loved, seen, and lovable—right now—because of Christ. The overwhelm, the despair, and the dark does NOT get to define us; Christ has bull-dozed the lies, has crushed the head of Satan, and has declared us perfect before God. Perfect in Christ is our new identity. Darkness is still present in our fallen world, but it no longer has power over us. No matter how bad things get, the love of Christ does not falter or abandon us. Nothing can separate us from the love of God that is in Christ Jesus (Romans 8:39), not our sin, not our worries, not our failed relationships or broken families, not bad grades, not sickness, not family members who get cancer, not the end of a job, not even our own death. The Gift of Christian mentorship is that we can remember together when alone is difficult.

What do we do with this Good News and new identity? Clothed in Christ, we freely love and serve our neighbor. In our relationships, we do this daily. *"We come before God clothed not in our own works or merits, but solely in the works and merits of Christ, which are imputed [credited] to us. But having been justified by faith, we are sent by God back into the world, into our vocations, to love and serve our neigh-bors"—Luther.* What is vocation, and why are we talking about it? We are called by the Gospel into various vocations or stations in life. Examples of our vocations can include daughters, students, friends, wives, workers, citizens, business owners, mothers, teachers, artists, and neighbors. Vocations embody what you do and where you are. And good news! Right where you are today, God works through you to serve your neighbor. We are free to do this because all the work for our salvation has been finished in Christ Jesus. We never need to fret over logistics; instead, we live according to God's will, and in peace, we rejoice in the Gospel wherever we are.

In the chapters that follow, you are freely invited into the pres-ence of women discussing their various vocations. They are clothed, like you, in Christ Jesus. Like you, their lives are full of highs and lows. They are not here to be pinups of perfection but to be a place where truth is shared and where, in relationship as fellow sisters in Christ, you are warmly welcomed to read, to rest, to be mentored, and to grow. They are vulnerable inside of their stories in order that God's extraordinary grace may be made clearer in your vocations.

They serve you, love you, and pour experiences out for you, calling you back to your new identity in Christ as we wrestle together with all that life brings.

So, what do you think of when you hear women mentoring women in the church? Clinging to our identity in Christ, we remember we are not actresses playing the role of perfect women who have it all together. We are women declared by God to be perfect and redeemed. The lies that act as brick walls separating us from each other and from God have been demolished. Instead, God builds our mighty fortress in His Son, and here we may rest. As sisters in Christ, we can listen, love, pray for each other's needs, forgive, support, invite, cry with, laugh with, play, and worship alongside one another, sometimes giving more, sometimes receiving more. Grabbing the hand of another and leading her to the Gospel truth that comforts her is the Gift Christian mentorship gives. Honestly, there will be times we may get it right, but there will be times we do not. Sinners interacting with sinners will still sin and be sinned against. Knowing we ourselves have been forgiven, we can be ready to extend forgiveness and grace inside these relationships. As we dive deeper into the vocations within this book, we remember our identity in Christ's finished work on the cross and His victorious resurrection. His finished work is our finished work. His victory is our victory! It's worth saying again because this is so contrary to how we as women normally think—perfection isn't the goal for mentorship (and it's not the goal of this book!). In our vocations, we are free to hold each other up in forgiveness and love, reminding each other of our new identity in Christ. It is here, fellow sister, that we can engage one another with conversation, connection, and encouragement. The Good News has won salvation, freedom, forgiveness, and hope, and grants us a new identity in Christ Jesus. We are a sisterhood, sharing struggles, growing in Christ, and finding comfort that the Good News is even better than we thought!

# On Balance

*Crysten Sanchez*

Regardless of time or space, every woman juggles a million different responsibilities every day. This is as true for women today as it's been true since time immemorial. Author Nora Roberts has been attributed with the concept of glass balls. Picture this: You've got your family, obviously. How about your work or the essay you need to get finished before your professor's deadline? Spiritual life should always be at the forefront. Housework and journaling are ever-present. Don't forget your best friend or even just the acquaintances that matter to you. These are all responsibilities, or different balls, you're juggling all the time. According to Ms. Roberts, what you need to do is decide which of those balls are rubber and which are glass. Is it possible for you to hold everything up in the air all the time? Absolutely not. So, since you can't keep them all afloat simultaneously, you need to decide which of those balls, if dropped, are rubber and will bounce. Which of them are made of glass and will shatter? That's how you decide. Which of your tasks, your priorities, matter more than the others? Those are glass. Hold them up. Anything else, you let bounce. It'll be there for you on the other side. This is how you achieve balance.

There is no end to the pressure and expectation placed on you to perform, never let anyone down, look great while doing it, and to balance it all. Do it all simultaneously and make it look effortless, regardless of how much time and energy you put into accomplishing all the tasks for everyone else. You're called on to be everything to everyone, whether it's your professors, your husband and children, your friends, or your work. It's exhausting, and it's actually impossible.

Here's the thing. The Church has a different vocabulary. We don't talk about juggling or bouncing, and we don't actually use words like *balance,* either. We don't buy into the lies of the world when the world tries to tell us what our priorities should be and how we should balance them. We use words like *vocation, neighbor,* and *Gifts.*

What if you were able to join the two? *Balance* your *vocations.* Live faithfully in the places and relationships to which you have been called by God. And know which ones are meant to be given more attention and focus than others. If you can get all of that just right, maybe it'll work out the way you want.

But vocations aren't meant to be balanced. That's not the point of vocation. God has something better. God actually accomplishes things through your vocations, giving Gifts where He chooses, through His people fulfilling their vocations.

The Lord uses His creation to care for His creation. This is how He has designed us to live in proximity with each other. We are all given to people to care for and are given people to care for us. This is vocation. Vocations are callings, different roles that you function in under the cross of Christ while you live in the world where God has placed you. They're masks of God, ways for Him to show Himself and the love He has for His creation through everything from the nurses caring for their patients to mothers loving their children while keeping them clean, housed, and fed, or the 65-year-old woman in the church who takes on the responsibilities of making sure funeral luncheons are scheduled and handled. God uses the things He created to care for the things He created.

You are a creation that God uses in order to care for His creation. You do this while you're living in your many vocations. You're a daughter, a mother, a friend, a worker, a volunteer, a student, a mentor, and so much more. When it comes time to live the life in front of you, it's not yours to decide what you'll prioritize and what you'll let lie. Minute to minute, sometimes those priorities are even changed before you. That's kind of the original point of the glass balls. There are times when your kids are just fine hanging out at home while you handle a work situation that came up. But will you be the mother who continuously prioritizes work over involvement and time investment in your children? Not if you understand that, in the end, those relationships with your children are glass balls, and it's your responsibility to train those children up in the way of the Lord.

Again, vocation and balance. Vocation will always be at odds with balance. Balance implies that if you just did everything right, made all of the right choices, and put everything in just the right places, fulfilling your vocations would feel as peaceful as you've always wished it would be. It would feel balanced. But particular vocations will always demand more, and we will always fail to weigh them perfectly. The Law shows us this: We will never live up to the perfect picture of a wife, mother, student, friend, sister, or worker. It's not us who find the balance that we every so often accidentally achieve anyway.

Some days, it all actually goes right. The morning kisses to the kids, sending them off to school with a smile, are followed by a productive day of work and a well-balanced meal served on the clean kitchen table. Then the kids have their enriching activities in the evening, which tire them out just enough to send them to bed with books read and prayers said, and you fall asleep thinking that maybe it's not as hard as it might seem.

Until the next day, when failure happens as you turn every corner. You yell too quickly, respond too sharply, and end up phoning it in with take-out pizza and a movie because you just. can't. function.

God uses even that. He is always producing and perfecting through the work that you are doing through your vocations. Always. Even in the imperfect, during the bad days alongside the good. It's a law/Gospel answer, which our minds aren't good at wrestling with because it doesn't fit into the nice little buckets we've created for ourselves in order to manage everything. But the grace that you have in Christ Jesus doesn't exactly fit into a bucket either.

> For this reason I bow my knees before the Father, from whom every family in heaven and on earth is named, that according to the riches of his glory he may grant you to be strengthened with power through his Spirit in your inner being, so that Christ may dwell in your hearts through faith—that you, being rooted and grounded in love, may have strength to comprehend with all the saints what is the breadth and length and height and depth, and to know the love of Christ that surpasses knowledge, that you may be filled with all the fullness of God.

Now to him who is able to do far more abundantly than all that we ask or think, according to the power at work within us, to him be glory in the church and in Christ Jesus throughout all generations, forever and ever. Amen.
Ephesians 3:14-21

He provides *abundantly* more than all that we would ask or think. That includes the strength to manage the day and the responsibilities given to them. And He wants to. *But because he is God, he claims the honor of giving far more abundantly and liberally than anyone can comprehend – like an eternal, inexhaustible fountain which, the more it gushes forth and overflows, the more it continues to give.* (Large Catechism III 56)

You'll fail. We all do. There's no doubt about it and no way around it. But thanks be to God that you, in all of your weakness, are one who has been claimed and made new in your Baptism to live another day and care for the things and people given to you to care for. You're one redeemed, created to live as a mask of God to the people around you in your many vocations, and He'll see you through it. Not just with some platitudes and helpful thoughts but with actual, real forgiveness for the places you fail. Forgiveness won by precisely one death on the cross, with Blood that covers even your worst days.

No, not balance. Baptismal, sanctified, vocational living.

# On Service

*Deaconess Sarah Longmire*

Dear Sister in Christ,

This letter is about service. But it's going to start with Jesus. Service starts with Jesus, not in a "what would Jesus do" action call, but as a joyful reminder of what Jesus has done, is doing, and will always do. When you start with Jesus, you get to consider the best perspective to view service. Service becomes a gift you get to walk in instead of a burden you must carry.

When you start with Jesus, you start with the work He did for you. Jesus died on the cross, defeating sin and the devil. Jesus rose on Easter, killing death. You get to consider how you receive these gifts; in your Baptism, those victories are yours. In the Lord's Supper, you receive Jesus' Body and Blood. Good Friday, "it is finished" is for you. There are no extra tasks. There is no hidden agenda. You are redeemed, holy, clean, and enough in Jesus. This reframes how you can look at service! There is no "minimum requirement" of good deeds to "achieve." There is no secret bar that you just have to get to. Nope. Before God, you have the full, perfect pardon won for you by Jesus. This is indeed a freeing truth. You can take a deep breath and know that you are enough.

In Baptism, you are given the Holy Spirit. Jesus also promised to be with you always. You are never alone. In the Divine Service, you remember your Baptism, hear the Absolution of your sins, hear God's Word spoken, and eat Jesus' Body and Blood. He is with you as He promised. This is another amazing truth. In your moments of insecurity, struggle, suffering, and pain, you have the loving and merciful presence of God. This gets to be the foundation of your approach to service. Jesus is working in and through you now.

Service does not have to be complicated. Consider the comfort you have received by the presence of a loved one; you are reassured that you are not alone. In the same way, your presence can be that for someone else! When you think you are just sitting with someone, not offering anything but your attention, you are providing a gift. You may not feel as though you are doing much, but being the reassuring presence for your neighbor in their hardest moments, whether it is your toddler who is throwing a tantrum about their snack or an elderly church member who is in hospice, you get to be Jesus for the person in need. This helps you better understand how to look at service. It can often feel heavy or uncomfortable, or it can feel boring and regular, but it is good. Service can be offering presence to those who are lonely or alone; God created us for one another.

At creation, Adam and Eve were created in God's image and were declared very good. You, too, are created in God's image, and in Jesus, you, too, are called very good. You are uniquely gifted and blessed as you. Specifically, as a woman, you have abilities and opportunities that will be unlike any other. You have vocations—roles and responsibilities—that God has specifically created for you. This truth has great depths. YOU were created in God's image. YOU have the gifts, talents, abilities, interests, and opportunities that are unlike any other. It is important that YOU are here.

As you consider your uniqueness, try not to compare with those around you. I get it; it's hard. Their gifts seem so much... Better? Cooler? Shinier? Necessary? And yet, you get to be you. It is very good. God's Word reminds you that God created you with intentionality; not everyone can be the hand, eye, or foot...some people are the elbow or the pinky. And yet, thanks be to God that each and every person is individually included in the Body of Christ and equipped to serve. Many members make up the Body; you are included, too.

Service is what you get to do for your neighbor. Service is how you get to use your unique gifts and talents, as given by God, to love and care for those around you. Perhaps you will be given a husband or are already married. Perhaps you will one day be a mother, or you already have children. Perhaps you will be given the gift of singleness, and you enjoy family as an aunt or godmother. Family is the most intimate way in which you get to experience community; this is where you love your closest neighbors. And yet, service may not always "feel" like you think "service" should feel. You find yourself changing a diaper... again. You are preparing dinner... again. You are doing yet another load of laundry. And yet, God would call all the works you do for your neighbor "good." In fact, He would compare them to serving Jesus Himself.

Consider the incarnation of our Lord. Mary, as His mother, took intimate care of Him as He formed in her womb and grew into a man. She fulfilled great acts of service as His mom; from the outside looking in, they may have seemed "boring" or "routine." In truth, they were holy and good in the sight of God. In familial roles of service, you, too, get to be the one showing your Lord's love through the actions, as normal and ordinary as they may be, that you perform and complete for others.

Additionally, service gets to be done in a wider sense—beyond families. Perhaps you have an interest in serving in established roles within the church—as a deaconess, teacher, musician, church worker, nurse, social worker, missionary... thanks be to God. A cool word in Greek, *diakonia* means "service to others." This word is the root for the English word, "deaconess." The Office of Deaconess is a role uniquely held for women in the church to intentionally serve others. Deaconesses get to learn theology, study God's Word, study the church's doctrine, and facilitate intentional opportunities to love and serve their neighbors. This usually happens within a church congregation, a care facility, or on the mission field. Deaconesses are women theologians—what a gift! Women theologians study and continue to learn from God's Word; they intentionally deepen their understanding about how to best communicate God's love and mercy to others. These women get to work within the proper context of the Church, teach others about the love of Jesus, and offer acts of mercy to those in need.

And yet, there are many other intentional roles in which women do acts of service and show mercy to those around them. In these situations, it is as though these women, who are loving and serving their neighbor, are "small d" deaconesses. (Remember: *diakonia* means service to others!) Women in these roles are reflecting Jesus' love and mercy to those who need it. So, if your interests are in education, music, medicine, or finance… there are roles in these fields that can be opportunities for you to serve your neighbor. In any relationship or role you pursue, you are the person who gets to tell and show Jesus.

Women are uniquely gifted and placed to serve those around them. Whether you are tying a child's shoes, making a bed, writing a Sunday school lesson, sitting with someone in the hospital, or holding a baby for the tired mama next to you in the pew, rest and rejoice in the knowledge that God created and gifted you for this service. You get to embrace the vocational roles that you have been given; you can be sure that God has equipped you for the work and continues to be with you as He uses you for the care of your neighbor.

Just as we started with Jesus, let's end with Him too. Jesus promises rest for the weary and peace for the burdened. In the moments when service feels like work and the task lists are long… remember that you can also be the one who receives from your neighbor. You are part of the Body of Christ, and you are a beloved member of various communities (e.g., your family, your church, your neighborhood, your school, your place of work). You are not the whole Body or the whole community but a beloved part. So, even as you are uniquely gifted to serve and love others, receive service and love too. Receive opportunities to rest, sleep, play, and be shown God's love by someone around you. God is in control, your salvation is secure in Jesus, and you are enough in your Baptism. It is good for Deaconesses and deaconesses to allow others the opportunity to show them Jesus.

Start and end with Jesus. Service is a Gift that flows out of His work—for you and for your neighbor. You get to do it, and you get to receive it.

With love, as a fellow Baptized Child of God,
Deaconess Sarah

# On Coming of Age

*Jennifer Bane*

Dear girl,

This letter is for you. For the girl who plasters a smile on her face every morning before heading out the door but is deeply wounded and lonely on the inside. For the girl who is trying so hard to "have it figured out" but is floundering. For the girl who looks in the mirror but quickly shifts her gaze away because she cannot stand the sight of herself. I am writing this letter for you—I am that girl—the girl who is continuing to find her place in life as a Christian in this world. I see you, and Jesus is there with you in the mess. I am still trying to navigate this earthly life, but I have found comfort in the Scriptures and reminders of God's love for us in my daily life. I am sharing a few of these reminders with you to reassure you that you are not alone—we are all trying to navigate this sin-filled world. God is there with you in the mess, even when you feel like the mess.

## 1. You are Enough because He is Enough

When I was in first grade, I accidentally wore my mom's Crocs to school. This may not seem like a big deal, but let's just recap. In first grade, my feet were so large that I wore my mom's size eight Crocs to school without realizing they were not mine. That's how big my feet were in first grade. Thus began, at such a young age, the comparison game. "Why am I so much taller than everyone? Why do I have to order special jeans to fit my long legs? Why does she have it all together, and I'm just a screw-up?"

The devil loves to play the comparison game—to sneak into your thoughts. To remind you that you are broken, you are sinful, you do not have it altogether, you are not enough. Enough. That's a tough one to swallow. Enough what? Pretty enough, smart enough, put together enough… all of the above?

Enter Jesus. We are enough because Jesus is enough. God sent His only Son to live a perfect life so that we don't have to live it perfectly. Jesus took on every sin of ours, every comparison we make, every enough, and nailed it to the cross with Him. It is still our human, sinful nature to compare ourselves to others. However, instead of thinking, "Am I enough?" I like to think, "Who is my God?" My God is a God that loves me so much to send His only Son to take it all on the cross for me. To die a brutal, painful death for me, expecting nothing in return. Since Jesus is enough, I am enough.

## 2. You Are Set Apart

I graduated from college when COVID was still very much prevalent. My job interview was over Zoom, and I accepted the job before I even visited the town. I ended up finding an apartment in an unknown town that I only knew about via Google Maps. I began my job in a town where I knew no one and nothing. I remember showing up to my first day of work thinking, "What am I doing here? I don't belong here."

Those first few years were lonely, exhausting, and most of the time, thankless. I am a public school teacher and found myself spending many hours on lessons that went wrong and families, it seemed, that I could never please. One day, a parent asked if we could meet and discuss her child's progress at school. We sat down and had a conversation about her child, but at the end of the conversation, she asked me something that took me quite off guard. "How can I pray for you?" she asked. This took me quite off guard. As a public school teacher, I cannot publicly confess my faith within my job. Confused, I asked, "How did you know I was a Christian?" With a smile, she replied, "I can just tell." That stuck with me: She could "just tell." Like there was something about me that set me apart from others. That's because there IS something that sets us apart from the rest of this world—our Baptism.

In our Baptism, God marks us as his own. The Holy Spirit comes down and wraps us in white, blemish and sin-free. God has set us apart from this sinful world and reminds us that we are His own children. Therefore, we have a duty, a calling, to go out into this world and show God's love, grace, and mercy to others.

In my vocation, I show the love of God to my students each and every day. God placed me at that school because that's where I needed to be—to teach with the love of God in my heart. While I may not be able to outright speak about Christ in my job, I can still show love, compassion, humility, and grace to those I work with every day. 1 Peter 2:9 states, "But you are a chosen race, a royal priesthood, a holy nation, a people for his own possession, that you may proclaim the excellencies of him who called you out of darkness into his marvelous light." Be that light to others, pointing others to Christ.

## 3. There is Still Joy

I went and visited my hometown recently. I took a moment to walk through the city park. The drinking fountain, shaped like a lion, was still standing there like it was when I was a kid. The color was a little faded, and I couldn't help but smile as I reminisced on some of my childhood memories.

Oftentimes, this world can seem a little dull—just like the faded drinking fountain at the park. There is so much pain and suffering. As Lutherans, we talk a lot about suffering. Yes, there is suffering in this world because our world is riddled with sin. Yet, there is still joy. God points us to Him and His mercy and love in little things in our daily lives. Whether that be the sun continuing to rise every morning (even though the past week has been hard), a conversation with a member of your congregation you haven't seen in a while, or even just a cup of coffee. These are things and people God places in our lives to remind us of His goodness. Suffering is inevitable, but God uses people and things in our lives to point us to Him and remind us of His love.

Girl, this world is tough. The devil will continue to creep into your thoughts, making you doubt yourself and your God. Society will tell you that you are worthless, and you may feel like the days continue to drag on with no end in sight. When we take a moment to look around, we can see that there is still good in this sin-filled world. Lean on the people and things that God has placed in your life to point you to Him—your pastor, members of your congregation, your Baptism. As John 16:33 states, "I have said these things to you, that in me you may have peace. In the world you will have tribulation. But take heart; I have overcome the world."

# On Being a Wife

*Allison Hull*

It was the first spring day in Chicago of my freshman year in college. Being from Texas, I had never experienced the seasons in all their glory before. Fall had been wonderful, with its cool crispness slowly rolling in winter and huge, beautiful snowdrifts. Finally, winter gave way to spring, and everything was thawing out. Amy and I had come from Texas together and made fast friends with Nicole, a Floridian. My boyfriend, Chris, was from Georgia, so as the token Southerners, we decided to explore a frozen lake Nicole had seen that had a huge fallen tree in the middle of it. Jim was our token Northerner along for the walk.

At first, we just walked along the tree, throwing sticks and rocks at the frozen lake. Next came Chris's hat, which he bravely retrieved, showing us that the frozen lake could hold weight. We all then tumbled out onto the ice, pretending to ice skate and see how far we could make it from the tree. We quickly found areas that were not as white in appearance, and water came up when we stepped on them. We three girls wanted to test our theory that we could make it all the way to shore, walking on the black ice while the men stayed back. Step by step, we carefully made our walk, all three in a line. And then, one by one, I watched in horror as my friends dropped into the icy water. Before I could turn, I was under.

It was needles stabbing at my legs and arms. Quickly, my feet and flip-flops were stuck in the mud. I couldn't breathe because the shock of the cold water kicked all the air out of my lungs. I tried to pull myself out, but every time I pushed on the ice, it broke clean away from my arms. I was stuck, panicking, not able to find a way out. And then I felt a splash behind me. Chris had jumped in. It might have been brute strength, adrenaline, or both, but he took me under the arms, pulling my feet out of the mud and FLUNG me across the ice. I skidded far enough away to safety. He then stomped through the water, breaking the ice as he went, to get to Nicole and flung her out as well. I will never forget the helplessness I felt and then the joy of being rescued. He became my husband three years later.

Like many young girls, I always dreamed of my wedding. Playing MASH and other games made it seem like the men were interchangeable and up to chance. All I needed was to insert a nice guy, and my wedding dreams would become a reality. As adults, we know this not to be true. Still, society has backed this up with approval for multiple marriages, trying things out before being married, and the ability to not ever get married since it's just a piece of paper. Marriage isn't about finding a nice guy. God speaks to us about marriage in Genesis 2:20-24.

"The man gave names to all livestock and to the birds of the heavens and to every beast of the field. But for Adam there was not found a helper fit for him."[1] (ESV)

The NIV translation is, "But for Adam, no suitable helper was found." What does it mean to be "suitable"? The dictionary describes it as being "right or appropriate for a particular person, purpose or situation." (Oxford Languages[2]) So we as Lutherans pray that our Father in heaven would give us the clarity to see the right spouse just for us. Eve was suitable for Adam, and Adam was suitable for Eve. She was made from his rib, which protects his heart so that she might be as close to that organ as another human can. They are "suitable" to each other because she makes up for everything that he lacks and vice versa. Apart, they may be strong, but together, both are impenetrable to the devil.

The cliches go, "Marriage is a two-way street. It's a give-and-take. I give, and she takes." But why does God ordain marriage as good? Why do we feel a need to be married? From the very beginning, Adam felt alone. Surrounded by everything he could think of, no one

---

[1]  Bible Gateway.com
[2]  Google Dictionary from Oxford Languages, Oxford University Press

was "fit for him." He needed someone who would be next to him, not beneath him or ruling over him.

"So the Lord God caused a deep sleep to fall upon the man, and while he slept took one of his ribs and closed up its place with flesh. And the rib that the Lord God had taken from the man he made into a woman and brought her to the man. Then the man said,

> "This at last is bone of my bones
>      and flesh of my flesh;
> she shall be called Woman,
>      because she was taken out of Man."
> Therefore a man shall leave his father and his mother and hold fast to
> his wife, and they shall become one flesh." (ESV)

Adam didn't marry Eve just because he felt alone; Eve was now a part of his body. One flesh, one blood, united by God, they are promised to protect, to honor, to love, and to fit only to each other. The only way they can do this is through Christ. "God's promise of the Savior from sin and death can only unite them. With this promise, we can walk with God through life. Keeping in mind God's mercy and grace through His Son and the Savior of the world (John 3:16), the husband and wife are reminded to be merciful to one another (Mark 11:25)" (Dorothy Preus God's Gift to Mankind-Marriage[3]).

In marriage, we have been given a suitable man to support him in life. What, then, does the daily life look like of the devout wife with her devout husband? There are two things to keep in mind daily in marriage. The first is that a devout wife is given the ability to help her husband not to make the same mistake Adam made in Paradise. This is when he did not stop or hinder the serpent's sermon but sat by and watched as his beloved wife took the fruit and ate. Being like Eve is being the "helper" to their husband. A helper will raise up the one they are assisting, making them be as God desires him to be and keeping him walking in the way God intended (Ephesians 2:10). Raising up this person to be able to be the best man he can be. Using your given

---

[3] "God's Gift to Mankind—Marriage Marriage from the Perspective of a Christian Woman Preserving the Christian Home" Dorothy Preus

Gifts to assist and, yes, even sometimes rescue him when he might be failing. The devout wife's duty is to her one flesh, but since she cannot rescue him fully from the power of the devil, the second daily Gift of a devout wife for her husband is to forgive him and remind him of Jesus' love when he does fail and despairs of God's love for him.

Being a devout wife doesn't mean changing everything about yourself so that you may help your husband. After all, God gave you to each other the way you were created so that you might lift each other up and support one another when each of you fails. Just as you are both saints through Christ, you are both still sinners in need of God's saving grace. "When one fails to fear, love, and trust in God above all things, one cannot love another as oneself" (Dorothy Presu). Even in a devout marriage, sin, the devil, and all his demons like to whisper in your ear. There will be times of doubt, times of anger, times of despair, and times of feeling alone, even when together. This is the time the devout husband and wife cling to God's promise and His unfailing love, reminding each other of this every day, helping them, forgiving them, and, in turn, loving our suitable marriage partner because of Christ's love for us; loving them as one flesh, helping and supporting them in every physical need.

When I was in the freezing water, feeling the iciness pricking my muscles, I couldn't get out. I wasn't thinking properly, trying to find my own path but sinking faster. So also, you, by yourself, cannot rescue yourself from sin, death, the world, and the power of the devil. By yourself, you will sink down more in despair, sin, and loathing. Or you will justify your own actions, driving your own self-love and importance while pushing everyone else away, including your spouse. Christ is the only one who can rescue you. Christ has come and saved you and all of mankind. On the cross, Jesus claimed you as His own and took on all sin, even those that husbands and wives commit against each other. "There was no counsel, no help, no comfort for us until this only and eternal Son of God, in his unfathomable goodness, had mercy on our misery and wretchedness and came from heaven to help us... He snatched us, poor lost creatures, from the jaws of hell, won us, made us free, and restored us to the Father's favor and grace."[4] In marriage, husbands and wives NEED to be reminded of

---

[4] *Large Catechism* II.29 Tapert p. 414

this daily and hourly. They must have Christ and his eternal sacrifice as their focus. There is no devout, suitable husband or wife, no devout marriage without the death of Christ. For without the death of Christ, there is no forgiveness, no love, no devotion to God or each other. Marriage IS a give and take, giving and taking Christ daily in forgiveness and love. So, the priority in marriage must be a devotional life. Rooted in Scripture, you have the ability to help your husband by reminding him of Jesus' love for him. Together, this Scriptural unity brings together the both of you.

If you are waiting for a suitable husband, in the midst of planning your wedding, are in the first years of marriage, or are a weathered old couple of 18 odd years, know that Christ loves you. Christ takes you out of the muck and the paralysis, cradles you in His arms, and claims you as His child. Christ found a suitable helper in His bride, the Church. In this, we can see such loving devotion and sacrifice that we can emulate in our own marriage. And when we both fail, we can point to the cross and remember the forgiveness and love Christ gives every minute, every second of the day. You are Christ's, and He is yours forever. You are your husband's, and he is yours. You are suitable. You are more than enough, for you are forgiven, loved, and claimed by Jesus forever.

# On Singleness

*Erin Alter*

I am intelligent, brave, afraid, and curious. I love all the spices and all the colors (except for khaki and beige). I cook without recipes and knit sweaters in church. I am selfish and harsh. I make smart-aleck comments to the person sitting next to me in meetings. Sometimes, I make them to the whole room. I am trying to tame my temper, but it still gets away from me when I am driving by myself. I am the eldest child and grandchild. I am an aunt and a godmother. I am single. When I was growing up, I didn't have ambitions of becoming an astronaut, a movie star, or the president. Instead, whenever I pictured myself in the future, I was a wife and mother. The rest was pretty hazy.

That isn't how my life has turned out, and sometimes I grieve that. Sometimes, I settle into a funk, imagining what isn't. Occasionally, I have dug myself beyond that funk into a full-on bitter spell, wallowing in envy and resenting God for not doing what I want Him to do.

Marriage is a Gift from God, and He has not given that Gift to me. If I am brave, I will give voice to my disappointment in my prayers. "Why do I long to be a wife without any fulfillment? Why doesn't the desire diminish with time? Why do You give marriages to people who don't understand what it means to sacrifice for the other and end up breaking that precious Gift in divorce? (As if I truly understand this, never having struggled with it personally.)" Prayers like this don't have to be logical, just honest, and while not every one of these questions is fair, I have asked them all. More often, I have chosen the cowardly path, not daring to fling my sorrow and jealousy at the Lord who loves me and promises never to forsake me.

Instead, I have fermented those emotions into vitriol and applied that caustic brew to myself. "You are too quiet, too loud, too smart (too conceited!), too-too. And while you are at it, you are also not enough. You're not pretty enough, not outgoing enough, not girly enough, not Lutheran enough. Excessively insufficient."

Perhaps you have found yourself applying these words to yourself, too. Here's the thing: They are lies. They do not tell you the Truth. You are comparing yourself with some other standard that you have decided is ideal, but there is no objective best for any of these. I am quiet and loud and smart and conceited and single. None of these are my defining characteristics. My true identity was given to me at my Baptism. "We were buried therefore with Him by baptism into death, in order that, just as Christ was raised from the dead by the glory of the Father, we too might walk in newness of life" (Romans 3:4).

There is a real temptation, especially in the Lutheran Church— Missouri Synod (LCMS), to elevate marriage above all else. Don't get me wrong, marriage is a Gift from God, and it is a godly desire to want the good Gifts of God. Our relationships do help make us who we are, but it is your relationship to God that gives you your deepest identity. You are a child of God, purchased and won by the blood of your Savior, Jesus Christ. Do not disdain that essential truth by choosing to pine for what you have not been given. And when you do, repent.

Being a wife is a vocation given by God. Being single is also a vocation given by God. The vocation of singleness is not inherently permanent, though it could be life-long. If you are doubting that you have this vocation, there is an easy way to tell. Are you married? If the answer is no, then congratulations, you have been given the vocation of singleness! Do you wish that this wasn't your vocation? Well, it might not always be yours, but that doesn't change the fact that it is one of your vocations right now.

Vocations are all about serving your neighbor. Singleness offers a unique strength that most other vocations lack: freedom of time and resources. When you are single, if someone asks you to do something and you have the time and capacity, you can just say yes. You don't have to consider your husband's preferences or your kids' priorities; you can just do it. A wife and mother must give precedence to her husband and children, and that is right. But you have the freedom to prioritize the needs of your friends, your co-workers, your next-door neighbors, and even the strangers you meet at the airport.

Perhaps you are thinking, "But the Bible says, 'It is not good that the man should be alone.'" (Genesis 2:18) First, stop trying to use the Bible to manipulate God into doing what you want Him to do. This passage is a beautiful example of how God cares for His people. He did not want Adam to be alone, so He created Eve to be a helper fit for him. However, this does not mean that God is bound to provide everyone with a spouse, nor does He promise to do so.

Second, I have good news for you! You are not alone. You are not the only person on Earth. You are surrounded by family and friends and by your church. You have a community, and you are a vital part of the life of that community—and that includes your vocation of singleness.

Very few people are masters of anything from the start. Some might have a natural affinity for music or writing or diving. But we all improve with practice. I enjoy sewing and knitting. I have spent hundreds of hours learning those skills. People often tell me, "I could never do that!" True, but primarily because they have never taken the time to learn and practice. Patience and self-control are gifts, but they are also disciplines to be practiced. The vocation of singleness is a vocation that you can grow in while it is yours.

"Only let each person lead the life that the Lord has assigned to him, and to which God has called him" (1 Corinthians 7:17). Being content with the life that the Lord has given me is sometimes challenging. I make it harder when I fall into the trap of comparing my life with others or (even more seductive) comparing my actual life with my wished-for-life. Perhaps you do this, too.

Dear sister, your life is not small. The Gifts God has given you are not small. Do not be contemptuous of them. Your life is not something of no value. You are not something to be looked at with contempt. Something to be avoided. Something to despair of. The Gifts God has given me, the Gifts He has given you, are real and of value and not inferior to those He gives to anyone in His Church. God does not give measly Gifts, and He gave those Gifts to you because the Church needs them. The Church needs your vocation of singleness.

We can deceive ourselves into thinking that singleness is a punishment. "I'm too 'not enough,' and if only I were different and better, then God would reward me." No. God doesn't manipulate us with His blessings. He isn't withholding the Gift of a husband because He hopes you will improve in your eyeliner skills. He isn't waiting for you to earn a husband. That is not His way. "God shows His love for us in that while we were still sinners, Christ died for us" (Romans 5:8). God's way is grace. All of this endless self-obsession primarily serves as an excellent distraction from the truth: that before the foundation of the world, my Father chose me in Christ (Ephesians 1:3-6). If I get caught in the whirlpool of self-pity, then my eyes are not fixed on Jesus.

Live in the now, dear sister. Maybe you will marry someday, maybe you won't, but "maybes" aren't certain. Cling today to what is certain: Jesus. Open your hands and receive daily bread from your Father, not the bread for next month or next year—He will give that later. Today, He gives you daily bread. He also promises, "My grace is sufficient for you, for my power is made perfect in weakness" (1 Corinthians 12:9).

Live the life that God has given you today, and when you realize that you have curled in on yourself, focusing on your flaws and your dissatisfactions, repent. Kneel at the altar, open your mouth, and taste the forgiveness of sins. Your Jesus is sufficient.

# On Motherhood

*Rebekah Jenkins*

When my oldest son was a baby, he was not meeting his milestones. Now, if you are not a mother, you might not realize how big of a deal these developmental standards are. Besides being asked to grade your child on them at every single pediatrician appointment, they are also the biggest topic of conversation among new moms. Right after the first question, "How old?" The next question is always, "Oh, so are they rolling/crawling/walking yet?"

I have watched my son struggle with many skills that come so much easier to other children. The first was gross motor: He struggled to move well beyond the age at which most babies could crawl. He started physical therapy when he was one and quickly made progress. He learned to crawl a few weeks into therapy and was walking by the end of the eight weeks.

At age two, my son still was not talking, so we decided to place him in speech therapy. Week after week, the speech therapist came to our home and week after week, we were not seeing progress. After several months, the speech therapist mentioned she thought he might have a rare neurological motor planning disorder, one that makes learning to speak exceptionally difficult. As soon as she left, I, of course, googled this disorder to find out that many of the kids diagnosed with it are never able to speak. I immediately started to wonder if he would be able to do all the "normal" things you hope for your children—go to school, play sports, drive, get married, and have children.

It was so easy to catastrophize my two-year-old. Over the last five years, my son has had multiple diagnoses and has participated in speech, occupational, and physical therapy. We had to pull him out of daycare, and I had to change my job to provide what he needed to thrive.

Have I scared you yet? That is not my intention. My intention is to show you that motherhood is not all rainbows and butterflies. You probably already know that. Maybe you know that too well and have no interest in entering this vocation. Culture certainly does not paint motherhood in a positive light. There is a lot of sacrifice with what seems like very little reward.

Or maybe, like me, this is something you always wanted. You know it will be hard, but in the way things in the future tend to seem hard—abstracted and without any real knowledge. Of course, that would make sense because you do not know what kind of hard your motherhood will look like—you could very easily have children with no developmental delays, but maybe your kids will have neonatal ICU stays, allergies, not sleep through the night, wander from the faith, or loss of their own to endure.

No matter what your motherhood in the future looks like, we know that it will be in a sinful world. That's the one common denominator that unites motherhood among all faiths, backgrounds, and worldviews. Eve bit the fruit and the curse was put onto women: "I will surely multiply your pain in childbearing; in pain you shall bring forth children. Your desire shall be for your husband, and he shall rule over you" (Genesis 3:16).

All of this can be overwhelming: the fear of the unknown, the fear of messing up, the fear of the pain. Becoming a mother itself can be difficult and can include infertility, miscarriage, or infant loss. It can all be difficult and filled with grief.

Our families are Gifts from the Lord. If you are blessed with children, you know they are from the Lord, and their Father loves them and desires for them to be saved. "Behold, children are a heritage from the Lord, the fruit of the womb a reward" (Psalm 127:3). These children are temporary blessings from the Lord, and your job is to love them and point them to the Lord. When things are going poorly by worldly standards, you have the assurance from the Savior of everlasting life. He gave you the Gift of these children, and He will be with you while you navigate loving them. He cares for your children more than even you can; He knows the number of hairs on their heads, the number of their days, and their most treasured desires. You are not alone in motherhood; you are loved and cared for by your own Father in Heaven. When you are tired, anxious, and unsure, you can turn to Him with confidence that He loves you and desires what is best for you and your family.

Motherhood is just like any other path a Christian is to walk on earth—by daily contrition and repentance with the understanding that this is all temporary. You take the child to the waters of Holy Baptism as soon as you are able, and you begin to try to teach them about the perfect Savior that died for them. You sin against them; you repent. They sin against you; you teach them to repent. You will have other vocations during motherhood, and you will have to balance those other vocations—wife, daughter, sister, and friend. Those other relationships will hopefully also love your children and invest in their lives. These other relationships will be able to invest in you while you invest in your children and point out your sin so you can repent.

God constantly calls us His children, and we are to refer to Him as our Father. When you experience the Gift of motherhood, you will better understand how much the Lord loves you and desires your salvation, for you will experience a new kind of love and desire for the salvation of your own children. You were made a child of God in your Baptism, and you get to witness your own children become Children of our Heavenly Father. What a gift!

I am still early in my motherhood journey. God-willing, I still have many years left with these children in my home. I am constantly learning and growing in what my children need, and I expect that only to increase as they get older. I want you to know that motherhood is a great Gift and responsibility that the Lord has blessed us with.

If you are single and hope to one day have children, choosing a husband who will also teach your children about the Lord's faithfulness and Gift of redemption is of utmost importance.

Today, my son speaks and can be understood. He is still in speech therapy and likely will be for years to come, but he is one of the most resilient people I have ever met because he has already had to overcome so much. My husband and I constantly have to remind ourselves that the point of parenthood is not to hit all the milestones, participate in all the activities, have children that are the most put together, or have the best grades. The point of parenthood is, "Train up the child in the way he should go, and even when he is old, he will not depart from it" (Proverbs 22:6).

At the end of the day, all of this is temporary. Our goal is to raise them to be adults who love the Lord and, ultimately, die in the faith to be resurrected on the Last Day to spend eternity with our Father in Heaven.

# On Family

*Tana McKenna*

Greetings, dear sisters in Christ!

When I was asked to write this chapter, "On Family," my initial thought was that MY family was a hot mess! Why on earth would you want me to write about family?!?! I mean, on the outside, we look pretty good and fairly well-functioning; there is not a whole lot of dysfunction. But if you really get to know us and spend any amount of time with us, you'll see we've got some issues! As I contemplated where to go with this letter, I realized perhaps that's exactly the message you need to hear… family IS a hot mess in many and various flavors, and we all live in that hot mess! It may seem from the outside that some are more put together than others, with no drama, trauma, or angst. But that's usually just on the outside. Get to know anyone, and there is always some sort of varying degree of any or all of those things present.

That really doesn't seem very encouraging, does it?! But let's unpack this a bit and see where the abounding grace and encouragement can be found in the midst of the hot mess.

First of all, I want to be very clear that family means all sorts of different things to different people, and I am absolutely no expert on the social dynamics of family makeup or its implications in society. I'm just a daughter, wife, mother, and hopeful grandma. I've observed some things, lived some things, learned some things along the way, and I am here to share a few bits of those things with you. So please take what I have to say as just that: observations and maybe some wisdom from a woman who has lived and loved and learned. My prayer is that you will take these words as encouragement, advice, and something to reflect on. Nothing more, nothing less.

So family. There's the family we're given. Parents. Husband. Children. I've been blessed with a very traditional and relatively stable family. My parents, still together after 55 years and some real ups and downs, raised me and my sister on a one-earner, lower-middle-class income with just enough to be comfortable but not ever much extra. We didn't take vacations, have cable (or color!) tv, or the latest designer jeans. We camped in a pickup camper on the side of the road next to a trout creek in the middle of nowhere Montana with no electricity, no running water, and no toilet. Our shoes were from Kmart. We went to Grandma's house to watch Hee Haw on Sunday night. And honestly, we thought life was pretty great. Looking back, it was pretty redneck! But it laid the foundation for a motto that has been with me my entire life. Be Happy With What You Have. It was less than not much, but at the time, we didn't even realize how close to nothing we really had! My parents made sure that what we did have, we appreciated and didn't take for granted. Most importantly, we went to church together as a family. Every Sunday. No exceptions. No matter how much we fidgeted and squirmed as toddlers or whined and complained as teenagers, we were in the pew every Sunday. Did I get at the time how important this foundation was? Of course not! I had the typical teenager reactions… indifference, annoyance, pushback. But they never wavered, never compromised. Church was not negotiable. It was a part of who we were as a family and shaped and molded me to be who I am today.

Fast forward to Husband. I met Brian while we were in college. He was at the state school studying to be a mechanical draftsman, and I was at the private college studying religion and the classics, planning to go to seminary and be a pastor. What? Yep, you read that right. I was raised in a church body who believed that being a pastor was something women could, and were encouraged to, do. I didn't like science or math, I loved to read, and I cared about people, so that was the path I was encouraged to take. But the Lord had other plans. As we talked about our future together, Brian made it very clear that I was much more valuable to him as a wife and mother to our children and that by being a pastor, I wouldn't be able to do both. Pastor work is hard, and it's not given for everyone (especially women!) to do. What my sinful flesh heard was that he was going to work, and I could stay home and take care of the kids and not have to take on more debt with school and the responsibility of a career. I was all for taking the easy way out! He didn't really understand the weight or the reason behind his desire... he just didn't want to be the one wrangling a toddler in the pew while I was preaching or doing bedtime alone while I was at church meetings. Neither one of us understood that this was the Lord's design for marriage and vocation! It took us YEARS, and finally, we were taught by a faithful, patient pastor that marriage is given to us as a Gift and modeled for us in Christ and His bride, the Church. My vocation as wife and mother is part of that beautiful design, meant to honor and support my husband, who is willing to sacrifice everything for me and our family. What seemed like just a practical choice for us was actually a beautiful Gift! Now, because we're miserable sinners, most of the time, we function within that beautiful Gift as a hot mess. We fight over the laundry, yard work, and who controls the remote. We get our feelings hurt and offer the cold shoulder in return. We forget to tell each other important details and then are defensive and arrogant. We cry, we yell, we sulk, we ignore. But... we are steadfast in our commitment to be in God's Word together. That word, delivered to us by faithful pastors, continually turns us back to Christ—to his forgiveness, his bleeding and dying for our sins. And in that forgiveness, we, too, forgive. The hot mess is part of living in this sinful world, but the Gift of being grafted into the family of God is what holds us together.

Fast forward to children. Oh, children! They are a Gift of the Lord. And also, a burden we must bear. God definitely knew what he was doing when he increased women's pain in childbearing as a consequence of the Fall. That pain isn't just in the temporary of actual childbirth. It's a lifelong process! The sleepless nights, sickness (pukes in the middle of the night are something no one can prepare you for!), and stubborn determination (I can do it MYSELF!) of the early years. The sass, rebellion, broken hearts, and fights with friends of the teenage years. Will we come out of this alive? Through those early years, that was a very real goal—if everyone is still alive at the end of the day, we're doing ok. There was an arm broken by the older brother on a trampoline, a hand cut by dad with a slip of a hunting knife, and countless other close encounters that left us tired and cranky and at our wit's end. But at the end of the day, we sat down at the table together to pray and eat a meal, even if it was Kraft mac and cheese for the third time that week. We folded hands (sometimes in a wrestling move!) and said prayers at bedtime. And we went to church. Together. As a family. Those rambunctious boys knew that for an hour every week, they were expected to have their butts in the pew and pay attention. Would it have been easier to skip it? Absolutely! Were we perfect and never missed a Sunday? Nope!! But the expectation was there, and the foundation was laid that church was not just something that had to be done; it was a Gift! You didn't HAVE to go; you GOT to go. It was the thing that reset us at the end of a crazy week, refocused our eyes on the important things in life, and forgave all of the yuck. Now that my rambunctious little boys are young adults, about to become husbands and, lord willing, fathers themselves, my own faith is strengthened. They have sought out for themselves godly, faithful women to build their own families with. They take the task of being the head of their own household seriously. They still stink and make dumb decisions, but they cling to and live under the grace and forgiveness that they know is theirs in Christ Jesus!

So then, what's my encouragement to you? Do I have the secret? Is there a magic wand to wave and make all of the icky seem less icky? To have the appearance, at least, of being lovely and amazing? Or at least not a complete train wreck! No. No magic wand. No handbook. No task list or formula to follow. No secret. Christ is the answer. Only Christ. For through Him and with Him and in Him, you will find the abounding grace that carries you through. That grace is what brings joy and life to your family. Whatever family you have been given or grafted into. Keep Christ and his promise of forgiveness at the center of all you do through all the hot mess of the worst times. Keep Christ and his promise of life and salvation at the center of all you do through every milestone and life phase. Each stage, each phase of life, brings challenges and triumphs, failures and accomplishments, hardships and joys. Don't wish any of them away. Don't give in to the temptation of thinking that life will be better, easier, and perfect if we just make it through THIS phase. It won't. Nothing on this side of eternity will be perfect. I encourage you to have joy in your journey.

Grin and bear it through the hard stuff; rejoice in the good stuff. But live in it, constantly reminded that life is not about how good of a wife or mother or daughter you are. You will sin and fall short. But you have been grafted into the family of God, a sister in Christ, a child of the Heavenly Father. And the love, joy, peace, patience, kindness, goodness, faithfulness, gentleness, and self-control that are the fruits of the spirit are yours in Christ Jesus our Lord. The Gift of salvation and eternal life has been given to you in your Baptism, delivered to you in His Body and Blood, and poured into your ears through His Word. My hope for you is that you will live joyfully in that Gift.

# On Friendship

*Amanda Sturdivant*

"Be kind to one another, tenderhearted, forgiving one another, as God in Christ forgave you." Ephesians 4:32

What does friendship look like? I'm sure we all have movie-like images ingrained into our minds: sleepovers, coffee dates, shared belly laughs, companionship as we shed tears, living your entire life with the same tight-knit group of friends until the screen goes white and the credits roll on your lives. That's friendship… right? Well, those things could certainly be included, but let's zoom out and take a realistic look at what the Christian vocation of friendship is and what it requires of us.

"Many are the plans in the mind of a man, but it is the purpose of the Lord that will stand." Proverbs 19:21

Friendships are like planting a garden from scratch. First, you plant the seed—make a connection with a new person through similar interests and common ground. You water that seed—you get to know each other and become more vulnerable and trusting. You nurture the friendship until it begins to blossom, revealing new, exciting, complex layers. Your new friendship takes work to maintain. Sometimes, they grow and bloom years into the future; sometimes, they wither and fade. One of the most important vocations that God gives to us is that of being a friend. All relationships go through phases, and most don't last forever, but the time that we have with our friends is one of God's greatest Gifts.

> "What God ordains is always good: He never will deceive me; He leads me in His righteous way, and never will He leave me. I take content, what He has sent; His hand that sends me sadness will turn my tears to gladness." LSB 760 v.2

Do you still talk to your friends from elementary school? High School? Your first job? I've had some amazing friends throughout the course of my life that have truly shaped who I am. Some of the best friends I ever had were beside me as bridesmaids when I got married. Unfortunately, I cannot say that I am still in contact with all of them. If I were to get instead married today, I would choose different people to be in my wedding party. I'm a different person today than I was all those years ago. However, if I went back in time, I wouldn't change the five women that I chose to stand beside me for the world! God placed us together at that time and gave us the vocation of being friends to each other because we needed each other for that season.

> "For everything there is a season, and a time for every matter under heaven: a time to be born, and a time to die; a time to plant, and a time to pluck up what is planted." Ecclesiastes 3:1-2

Throughout our lives, we will go through many seasons, so we will have various unique vocations—daughter, sister, church member, student, employee, wife, mother, and more. Through these seasons, we will have friends that accompany us through each. We will have bridesmaids, roommates, coworkers, and more. God gives us friends for each of the seasons of our lives. Friends to cheer us on, hold us, support us, bear our burdens, and friends that need us to do the same for them.

> "This is my commandment, that you love one another as I have loved you. Greater love has no one than this, that someone lay down his life for his friends." John 15:12-13

Just like we have these different vocations, the vocation of a friend has different requirements, needs, and layers. Just like how these vocations have seasons, so do our friendships! We all give and receive love differently. The scale is oftentimes unbalanced. Sometimes, you need to be the friend who is selfless and listens, offering a comforting shoulder as a safe and stable resource with soothing words and sound advice. Sometimes, you are the friend that needs to word vomit and vent and get all the emotions out so you don't explode. You are the one who needs comfort and a hand to guide and strengthen you. You are the one who needs a listening ear and a shoulder to cry on. So you go to your person—your bestie, your buddy, that steady rock who knows and loves you. There is no shame in seeking solace in others. God specifically created Eve for Adam so that he would not be alone! God has given us the strength to bear our friends' burdens and point them to Christ so that they know that they are not alone!

> "Two are better than one, because they have a good reward for their toil. For if they fall, one will lift up his fellow. But woe to him who is alone when he falls and has not another to lift him up!" Ecclesiastes 4:9-10

A friendship is filled with selfless acts that show care for our neighbor. These works certainly do not save, but instead, they show Christlike love and support for our neighbor, just as we are commanded. Send a simple text, email, or phone call to let them know you were thinking of them. Purchase or create a gift that reminds you of them and you know will bring them joy. Lend a helping hand by cooking dinner, watching their kids, or running an errand for them. Make it a priority to spend quality time together without distractions or expectations. Embrace in a tight, squeezy hug, or hold hands. Putting our neighbor's needs before our own is an act of service and love, which will bring them earthly comfort in their time of need.

> "Do nothing from rivalry or conceit, but in humility count others more significant than yourselves. Let each of you look not only to his own interests, but also to the interests of others." Philippians 2:3-4

God has made us each individually unique so that we may help and love our neighbor when they are in need. To give advice, guidance, and comfort, and exhibit Christlike behavior. Throughout our lives, God gives us a variety of people for a variety of reasons, each with a beautiful soul that impacts us and shapes who we are. Though you may not relate perfectly to each other or truly know firsthand what they're experiencing, you know your friend. You know how they think, how they feel, how they need to be loved and comforted, and you know that true comfort comes from the Gospel and Christ crucified.

> "Blessed be the God and Father of our Lord Jesus Christ, the Father of mercies and God of all comfort, who comforts us in all our affliction, so that we may be able to comfort those who are in any affliction, with the comfort with which we ourselves are comforted by God." 2 Corinthians 1:3-4

Here's the reality check... There are no perfect friendships; we are not perfect beings. Satan finds his way into relationships of any kind, and friendships are no exception. Conflicts happen in friendships, and there are times when you will feel alone, completely separate, or disconnected from your friends. Friendships are made up of sinners. There are no perfect people in a friendship. You will be wronged, and you will do wrong. You will hold them up, but they won't be there to catch you. They will call, and you won't answer. You will fail each other repeatedly.

> "When the righteous cry for help, the Lord hears and delivers them out of all their troubles. The Lord is near to the brokenhearted and saves the crushed in spirit." Psalm 34:17-18

The only way to be a good friend is to model yourself after Christ. Put on Christlike behaviors to care for your friends—carry their burdens with and for them, forgive, love unconditionally, and point them to the Gifts of Christ. Christ alone is perfect, and He sets the perfect example for us on how to treat our neighbors. We are given to forgive our friends who have wronged us, just as Jesus instructed. We are given to ask forgiveness from our friends because we will wrong them! We are sinners all!

"Put on then, as God's chosen ones, holy and beloved, compassionate hearts, kindness, humility, meekness, and patience, bearing with one another and, if one has a complaint against another, forgiving each other; as the Lord has forgiven you, so you also must forgive. And above all these put on love, which binds everything together in perfect harmony." Colossians 3:12-14

When we face those mountains of struggles, what you (and your friend) will need is a sister of faith to remind them that they are loved, they are not alone in this world, and that their struggles, pains, and faults are covered in the blood of Christ. They are not the ones responsible for their salvation! Guide them to hold fast in their faith, find comfort in their salvation through study, and remember their Baptism. Take them to church and pray with them. Invite them to Bible Study. Make time to share and discuss a devotional. No matter what, Christ has won the forgiveness of their sins and brings them eternal salvation. He is the ultimate comfort.

"Lord of all kindliness, Lord of all grace, Your hands swift to welcome, Your arms to embrace: Be there at our homing, and give us, we pray, Your love in our hearts, Lord, at the eve of the day." LSB 738 v.3

Through Jesus' sacrifice and love, we are shown what it is to be a friend. He is where we truly find comfort and guidance. He is the true example of the self-sacrifice that friendship requires. No matter what seasons our friendships go through, we can rest assured in our faith that we will never be alone, abandoned, or forgotten but always forgiven and saved. The challenges of this sinful world and our sinful flesh cannot take away the FACT that Christ was crucified for you, for your friends, and for us all!

"It is the Lord who goes before you. He will be with you; he will not leave you or forsake you. Do not fear or be dismayed." Deuteronomy 31:8

Your friend in Christ,
Amanda Sturdivant

# On Parish Life

*Deaconess Jeni Miller*

You don't get to choose your family.

For better or for worse, your family is given to you as a gift. You're born or brought into it. You grow to love it. You learn to live within the family, to be a part of it. You kind of… get what you get.

Can you see where I'm going with this?

The Lutheran parish is made up of people who are all very different. Of course, there is a range of ages, infant to elderly, and a mix of both men and women. There are mathematicians, nurses, engineers, students, and every occupation in between. There are the extroverts and the introverts, athletes and musicians, the quick-witted and the gentle, all sitting side-by-side in the pew and mingling together after the service.

It's unlike anything or any place else in life because nearly everything and everywhere else revolves around interests, hobbies, and shared experiences. But the Gospel isn't merely an interest. Church isn't a hobby. And our salvation in Christ is more than just a shared experience.

It's life.

That's why it's called a "church family," and the parish feels like an extension of home. We are all gathered together around Christ and

His Gifts, our source of life itself. It's a common faith, a common life, that unites us.

We're brought into these families for a reason. Like our Lord says in 1 Corinthians 12:18-20, "But as it is, God arranged the members in the body, each one of them, as he chose. If all were a single member, where would the body be? As it is, there are many parts, yet one body."

We're placed into our parishes to serve, to love, and to be served and loved. It sounds great, doesn't it? But let's consider reality for a moment. Family life isn't often easy. Because we are all so different, we don't always see eye to eye. Personalities clash, feelings get hurt, and sometimes it feels like life would be better if we just joined a different family. While it's true that life is more interesting and beautiful because of how God gathers unlikely people together, it can also be more difficult.

In short, sin gets in the way of parish life.

I've been part of many parishes in my life, and my role in those families has changed over the years. In two churches, I served as a deaconess. In two, I've been known as the pastor's wife and a mother of one, then two, then three, and four children. And in all of them, I've been considered relatively young, as part of the 40-and-under crowd.

Some of those churches were very adept at cultivating a rich and joyful parish life—what a blessing! In others, there were struggles—still a blessing!

You see, family life is always worth it. Even through the struggles, the Christian life is made richer and more beautiful. Through challenges, we learn an important lesson: Love the person in front of you as Christ loves you. Love and serve the church you have, not the church you want. Be a part of the family you have, not the family you want.

As with any family, joy can be found when we are grateful for the gift we've been given. It's important to intentionally give thanks for the mosaic that God creates when He sets us into families, both in the home and within His Church. Part of being thankful, too, is realizing that in our imperfections, our family loves us, too.

That's right. We're no perfect family members, either.

If you're part of a parish, it's a certainty—you will make mistakes. I've made my fair share of mistakes in every role, in every parish. The sooner we admit that we are just as likely to be the problem child in the family as anyone else, the better.

Here's the secret: Repenting of our pride and receiving Christ's forgiveness is key to a happy, healthy parish life, no matter what kind of church family you find yourself in. Be humble. (This is a big one.) Be patient. Be kind. Be meek. Be a peacemaker. Let's face it: The stereotypical stubborn church lady idea can be funny, but in reality, living that way can create unnecessary division and disorder. Instead: humility, humility, humility.

And when you fail, cling to Christ. Receive forgiveness from Him. Gratefully receive forgiveness from your church family, and be quick to dole it out to them, too.

The reality is that living as part of a Christian community—especially today—takes intentional work. It takes countercultural work. You have to choose not to be offended constantly. It requires you to be wise beyond your years, which means you'll be purposely seeking out faithful Lutheran women who are wise because of their years steeped in God's Word. Parish life means looking for opportunities to serve in a million small, ordinary ways.

After all, it's those ordinary moments that build up family and parish culture in a lasting way.

Because our parishes are made up of so many different types of people, we truly need to change our idea of what friendship looks like. Remember, it's not just about common interests, similar hobbies, and shared life experiences. It's deeper than that. We're friends in Christ; we're family because we know we will spend an eternity together. An eternity. Together. All because we are members of Christ's body. With that in mind, does it really matter that we don't seem to have everything (or anything) in common with each other aside from our faith?

We can love and serve each other—regardless of age, occupation, or even personality – because we have *the* most significant asset of life in common. We have Christ. That's why your parish—especially in our anti-Christian culture—is and should be your life source, your stronghold, and increasingly so. It has Christ as its foundation, so it cannot fail.

So take heart, ladies.

Sometimes, family life—parish life—looks... unattractive. Parishes may be small. Everyone may be old. You may not have a full-time pastor. The church might not boast an incredible music program or youth group opportunities. There may be people that you don't particularly like or who embarrass you.

Just. Like. A. Family.

But there's more to it all than meets the eye. Think of it this way. In the Divine Service, there is more to the liturgy than meets the eye. We worship with angels and archangels and all the company of heaven! Well, there is more to our parish life than meets the eye, too. We are connected as brothers and sisters in Christ. We are loved and cherished by Him. We are His. We are all—together, with those same angels and archangels and all the company of heaven—part of His Body, the Church. A family chosen by God Himself. And that is a great place to be.

So, parish life? It's the best life. Live it joyfully.

# On Embracing Stereotypes

*Magdalena Obersat*

"A new commandment I give to you, that you love one another: just as I have loved you, you also are to love one another. By this all people will know that you are my disciples, if you have love for one another." John 13:34-35

Lord, your mercies are new every morning. Let today be a testament to your loving kindness through the words from our mouths and the actions we partake in. May we live and love the way You have intended us to do and live the Christian life to the best of our ability. We thank and praise You for Your life, death, and resurrection. Amen.

Dearest reader,

> What's with the long skirt? Don't you know that's SO homeschooled of you? They went out of fashion years ago.
> Why are you waiting till marriage? You're completely bombing the vibe check.
> Why are you always talking about Jesus? You're trying to force your religion on me.
> You're pro-life? You must hate women.
> You're anti-gay? You're so hateful.

Wow. You really are a horrible person, aren't you? Welcome to the real world—it isn't what you expected. Last time I checked, they were all good, right, and salutary...

Or maybe... we aren't living in the real world after all. . . .

Stereotypes are completely unreasonable, right? They portray us as angry, hateful, and cruel. An article by Sage Journals says that the most common stereotypes of Christians can go in two different directions. Christians are said to be kind, charitable, and conservative, yet judgmental, hypocritical, and pushy.[1] Insert clip of angry screaming people. Sound familiar?

As I'm sure we Christians can all say, most of the others we know are the kindest people we've ever met. Unfortunately, that's not always the case. Since it's the extreme, guess what's going to be talked about the most? The loudest voices aren't always right. Welcome to Planet Sin.

To those outside of the Christian faith, we are stereotypically seen as crazy as someone trying to convince us chocolate syrup is the only ice cream topping. (I know it sounds crazy but stay with me here!) We argue that there is also caramel, strawberry, or none at all. We love our chocolate sauce so much that we want our family and friends to love it as much as we do. Sometimes, our combinations are different, making us hostile and unkind to those who put cherries or nuts on their frozen dessert and, more importantly, those who love chocolate and who avidly eat it plain...We love our pure, unadulterated Gospel, no matter how often someone tells us there are other options. It doesn't matter to us; we know what's true, good, and best. Understand the picture? Dessert opinions aside? Good.

We aren't talking about ice cream, though, are we? In our case, there is one right answer. These "extreme" stereotypes follow us because we are so passionate about the Gospel. The Lord is our incredibly gracious Father, and we long for a sibling to share in our joys. There are more people to enjoy family trips with, celebrate birthdays with, and even go to when things get tough. We want to share that unfailing love of Christ with those who have not come to know the Lord or who have chosen to fall away. That fear of a lost loved one can take over anybody. Maybe you or someone you

---

[1] Erentzen, C. A., Bergstrom, V. N. Z., Zeng, N., & Chasteen, A. L. (2023). The gendered nature of Muslim and Christian stereotypes in the United States. Group Processes & Intergroup Relations, 26(8), 1726-1749. https://doi.org/10.1177/13684302221138036

know have lost someone you loved—maybe in a car accident or to cancer. We're SO afraid to lose people that we allow fear and anger to take over when we're trying to convert that we forget they are people with emotions, too. Unfortunately, our sinful flesh tries to convince us at times that we should keep all of the gifts and trips and love to ourselves without giving those on the outside a chance.

This makes sense when we are lumped together in the modern eye as judgmental, pushy, and hypocritical, then… If you haven't figured it out yet, as people living in a sinful world, it is really common to sin. Like, a lot. One could lean on the verge of seeming "judgmental" because of our (mostly unbeknownst) habit of thinking we're better than everyone else. It doesn't look the same in everybody! Perhaps this "habit" is something you're blind to! (I usually don't realize it either until after a situation has passed.) It happens more often than you may realize.

While we are positively seen as charitable in many contexts, we are often depicted as rich and greedy because of media, televangelists, and mega-church leaders like Kenneth Copeland and Joel Osteen. In the TV show Young Sheldon, The Big Bang Theory's main character, Sheldon Cooper, receives a backstory of growing up in East Texas. The family's pastor is portrayed as hypocritical, scheming, and a thief. He steals money from his wife, lies to her about being rich, and shuns the Cooper family when their oldest son and his girlfriend are expecting a baby out of wedlock. A show like this receives incredible views and positive feedback, having a 7.7/10 on IMDb[2] and 86% positive feedback from Google user fans.[3] Based on these rates, it is more than plausible to say that people are influenced by this portrayal of Christians as a whole, particularly clergy members.

Somewhat fortunately, other forms of media show us to be family-oriented—praise God! In the pro-choice world, though, that's despicable, and we're seen as encouragers of "forced birth" and haters of women's rights. Why?? Why is it so terrible to embrace

---

[2] "Young Sheldon." *IMDb*. IMDb.com, September 25, 2017. Last modified September 25, 2017. Accessed September 26, 2024. https://www.imdb.com/title/tt6226232/.

[3] "Young Sheldon." *Google Search*. Google, n.d. Accessed September 26, 2024.

this beautiful command of being fruitful and multiplying? It's not "old-fashioned"; it's Christian. (Gen. 1:28). We share that we are known and loved before we were born.

> "Before I formed you in the womb I knew you, before you were born I set you apart; I appointed you as a prophet to the nations." Jeremiah 1:5

> "For you created my inmost being; you knit me together in my mother's womb. I praise you because I am fearfully and wonderfully made; your works are wonderful, I know that full well. My frame was not hidden from you when I was made in the secret place, when I was woven together in the depths of the earth. Your eyes saw my unformed body; all the days ordained for me were written in your book before one of them came to be. How precious to me are your thoughts, God! How vast is the sum of them! Were I to count them, they would outnumber the grains of sand—when I awake, I am still with you." Psalm 139:13-18

With this knowledge, it's more than a joy to support the traditional nuclear family and children as a whole! We wish that all would come to know that they're not alone and have been that way since before they began. We aren't ignorant of the horrible state of the world; we rejoice that we are not alone in the suffering!

Of course, our approach to taboo issues is the most prevalent image of Christianity, as we see with "forced birthers" and in being "hateful" towards homosexuality. (ahem-Mean Girls opening-ahem.) The verse we looked at in the beginning is often misquoted and used to justify acts contrary to God's Word, making it all the more necessary for us to preach the Word with the love of a sibling. It's so easy to be angry and feel a sort of hatred towards something we don't have to deal with ourselves. Sadness for things apart from God, however, is more than welcome. You have heard it said, "Hate the sin, love the sinner," and I would encourage you to do so. Hate is a pretty strong word, friends. Let your narrative be a broken heart from sadness. A sadness that someone's child has rejected its family. Let your love as a sibling shine through the pain. When you encounter someone struggling, remind them Whose they are and do your best to bring them home.

Take heart! There is Good News—always! Traditional values are Biblical. Traditional families, traditional worship, traditional masculinity and femininity... why do we think they exist in the first place if not for some greater purpose? (Let's not talk about those traditional tree-worshipping pagans...that's a problem for another time.) Within Christianity, we can guarantee almost 100% of the time that our Lord played some sort of hand in it. Contemporary Christianity holds the Bible as the lowest possible basis of their religion. Their "knowledge" comes from feelings, not Scripture. While your feelings are valid, let's not forget what Proverbs 3:5-6 says: "Trust in the LORD with all your heart and lean not on your own understanding; in all your ways submit to him, and he will make your paths straight."

Look at megachurch preachers like Joel Osteen, who we mentioned before. They hardly ever open their Bible and beg you to give them more money!

We traditional Christians, traditional Lutherans, have the exceeding joy in knowing that where the Word is, there He is also, and what better a place than in the most beautiful traditions this world has seen! We understand that our first priority is to make sure we keep our hearts turned to the Father, putting Christ first in our lives. We are consistently tempted to make choices that platform ourselves. I want my clothes to show I fit in. I want to be noticed, to be loved, to fit in, and I'll do pretty close to anything to do so. But dear sister, when you value the mentality of fitting in over being stewardesses of God's love, you aren't really practicing what you preach. Who do you love more? Yourself, or the one who gave you life? Just because these so-called "ancient traditions" seem out of style and make you look crazy does not mean that they are any less beautiful. You are more than welcome to be trendy and use that for His glory! The inside HAS to reflect the outside, or else people won't know they can trust you. Never doubt that you are beautiful because you live in the reflective rays of Christ's light.

So, why, dear sister, are you so hated? Why does the world laugh at you and blame beautiful you for its problems? Our so-called "judgments" are based on Biblical texts that tell us what is godly vs. what isn't. We are told to use wisdom when discerning right from wrong and to cast out the evil in our lives. That is what is seen as judgmental. Choosing modesty because we preserve ourselves is seen as judgmental when taken the wrong way. Choosing to stand up for the voiceless is seen as judgmental because we are judging someone else's way of life… choosing to have a conversation about the Biblical basis against homosexuality because we believe in Sola Scriptura… these "judgmental," these "conservative," these "traditional" things, controversial or not, are what aids us in living a Christian life.

Readers, I encourage you to embrace the stereotypes of being the kindest, most heartfelt, and most charitable people. Do not shy away from beautifully handling tough issues that the Lord has given us the grace to. Praise Him for the Gift of the Word and the promise of salvation that inspires the love in our hearts! May they be ready and willing to spread this Gospel to all nations and embrace everything that makes us who we are in Him!

With love,
Magdalena, your hopeful sister-in-Christ!

# On the Politics of It All

*Deaconess Ellie Corrow*

It can be difficult to live as a faithful Christian woman in this world, and sometimes the church makes it even harder. Does it surprise you that I would say that? We expect the culture, however we're defining it, to pressure women to give up their fidelity to Christ and His Word, but the church shouldn't be an obstacle to faithfulness. Properly speaking, of course, the church isn't an obstacle to faithfulness, as she preaches Christ's Words of Law and Gospel, administers The Sacraments, and strengthens us as we walk in danger all the way. However, theological language can be weaponized in service to many causes, and in a climate where gender roles need clarity, it can be tempting to build a reactionary theology about the roles of women that speaks beyond the bounds of Scripture. This creates false burdens on women and cultivates conflict between men and women.

Perhaps you have seen the countless articles, books, and podcasts that catalog appropriate parameters for women by extolling the virtues of so-called "biblical womanhood." These resources are ostensibly a correction to the excesses of feminism and govern everything about women, from their professions, education, hobbies, clothing, hairstyles, voting habits, and even speaking voice, all under the guise of retaining feminine submission. According to recent literature, the ideal "biblical woman" should be married and have children; she should not work outside of the home, much less have a career; she should not waste her time or fertile years on education, and in some circles, she probably shouldn't vote. Of course, there is nothing wrong with a woman choosing to adhere to these standards, as marriage,

children, and homemaking are all good, godly endeavors that should
be encouraged! However, the trouble is when this lifestyle is described
as the only acceptable, faithful path for women, it creates the expectation that women only occupy certain spaces in certain ways, and devi-
ations from those expectations are treated with outsized suspicion.

Clearly, all of us, male and female, should strive to conform
to Scripture's various admonitions and prohibitions. But have you
noticed recently how admonitions for disciples are so often gendered? For example, submission and meekness are seen as feminine
traits when all Christians are called to submission and meekness,
not just women. In Numbers 12:3, Moses is described as meek; in
2 Corinthians 10:1, Paul describes Jesus as meek; in Colossians 3:12,
he tells all of us to be meek. Meekness is obviously not particular to
women. Similarly, if we look at submission, all Christians are commanded to submit to authorities in Romans 13 and 1 Peter 2, and
there are several other ways Christians are told to submit to those in
vocational authority over them. Yes, Paul does tell wives to submit to
their husbands, but again, that is in the context of vocation and does
not extend female submission to all men. Both men and women are
to submit within their contexts, so there is nothing uniquely feminine
about submission.

In reality, the idealized quiet, submissive, and meek femininity
so often espoused within the church is itself as much a product of
culture as the feminism that it rejects. Femininity exists not outside
of women as some aesthetic or behavior but exists in our bodies that
were created and redeemed as female bodies. Femininity doesn't
reside in the length of our hair or hemlines or the amount of pink
or glitter we prefer but is rooted in our physical bodies. Women are
feminine because they are women. For many women, the expressions
of their femininity are different, as we are each individual humans,
created and redeemed by our Lord.

We can see the reality that Jesus makes us all different just by
looking around our communities, workplaces, schools, or even our
own families. While still remaining women, some are tall, some
are short, some petite and fine-boned, and some are remarkably
strong. Some women like cars, some love weightlifting, others love
cross-stitching, still others love to cook, and some love all of these
things. Our differences are part of our humanity that is redeemed

and sanctified by our loving God. God doesn't call his people into bland uniformity; rather, He takes our createdness and sanctifies it for fulfillment in creation. As we navigate life in this fallen world, it can be tempting to respond to things out of fear, to seek conformity and narrowly defined vocations we weren't made for. Or maybe not made exclusively for. Even as we look to Scripture, we see women who were business owners, women who were mothers, women who were midwives, women who were prophetesses and judges. None of these women are corrected for their vocations—instead, they used the Gifts given to them by God in His service and in the service of their neighbors.

The story of Jesus visiting Martha and Mary is a familiar story. Martha welcomes Jesus into her house but is busy and distracted with her work (many imagine the work of hospitality). She is soon frustrated with her sister, Mary, who, instead of helping, is sitting at Jesus' feet. When Martha suggests that Jesus correct the situation, Jesus instead offers his corrective—"Mary has chosen the better part" (Luke 10:42). A lot of Bible studies, especially women's groups, have spent an enormous amount of time dissecting this passage because it seems to stand as a corrective to theologies that have perhaps overemphasized hospitality as exclusively the holy work of women. You see, Mary had taken a place at her master's feet, the place of a student; it made no difference at all that she was a woman. There was not a separate "female discipleship" place for Mary; she was shaped by the Word of her Lord, just as all Christians have been from the beginning of time. Perhaps this seems an obvious statement but given all the time that is spent on overlapping concepts of "biblical womanhood," I suspect it is not as obvious an observation as we would suppose. I'm certain it's a familiar passage to you, and a lot of ink has been spilled to get Jesus to say not quite what he seems to be obviously saying. Martha's doing the expected quiet, demure, domesticated thing. She's doing exactly what would have been expected of her as a woman, and let's not be too hard on her for trying to provide a meal for our Lord, but she does kind of miss what Jesus is doing, doesn't she? What is he doing? He's addressing Mary as a disciple. Mary is seated at the feet of Jesus, which is the place of a disciple, and her womanhood doesn't keep her in the kitchen; it's welcome where all disciples are—male or female.[1]

---

[1] I am indebted to Dorothy L Sayers for this insight.

Let us turn to another biblical woman who you're perhaps less familiar with—Huldah the Prophetess. Who? We meet her in 2 Kings 22 and 2 Chronicles 34 during the reign of Josiah. Josiah wants to be a faithful king, so he commissions repairs on the temple, during which the builders discover the Book of the Law of the Lord given to Moses, and in reading it, they repent of their sinfulness. Josiah then commands his priest and additional staff to inquire of the Lord by sending them to Huldah, the prophetess. This is an interesting moment in the gender politics of their day and ours. The king and his priest sought counsel and submitted, if you will, to the words of a prophet who happens to be a woman. She was trusted to know the word of the Lord and to speak it faithfully, regardless of station, status, or sex.

It strikes me that so many of the ideals of "biblical" womanhood strive to make women smaller and quieter. Much like Victorian children, they are to be seen and not heard. We will know of the presence of a woman by the evidence of her labor and not by the demands of her voice. Certainly, there is a time to learn in silence and submission. Paul explicitly commands it in 1 Corinthians 14, yet even in silence, women are to be like Mary and learn at their master's feet. However, silence is not the totality of what is expected of women, as we see with Huldah. She was called upon to speak the word of the Lord and did so, even when her words were condemning. In the Scriptures, we meet women who used their voices, their social capital, their financial capital, and their prayers to advance the cause of the Gospel. These women are as varied as the women we meet today, but what bound them together was the love of their Lord and faithfulness to His Word. It would be surely easier if God had given us a straightforward playbook for each situation as we try to navigate the differences between men and women in society and the church, but instead, we're asked to walk together in mutual submission, meekness, grace, and forgiveness, as we seek to serve our Lord and each other faithfully. This way is not without its frustrations, of course, but in your frustration, don't reach for silence because you think it is what your God demands of you as a Christian woman. There will be times for silence, but there will also be times to use your voice and to take up space, knowing that the Lord has called other women before you to do the same.

# On Having a Voice

*Dr. Bethany Kilcrease*

You have a voice. Whether you are able to physically speak or not, you have a unique voice with something to say to the world. But this is something most girls (especially my own) and young women already realize. In addition to being a wife and mother, I have the vocation of college professor. In that capacity, I get to spend a lot of time talking with young women. Guess what? They almost all know they have voices, but what they really struggle with and wonder about is what exactly their authentic voices are. Just what makes one teenage woman's voice different from any other person's voice? And how do you know? How can you be sure you've peeled back the false layers of self your family or society has smothered you with so that you can uncover your true voice? Finally, once you've discovered what you think is your true voice, how do you best convey this to the rest of the world?

The struggle to answer these questions leads to no small amount of stress on the part of my female college students, in particular. Who am I? What is my real voice? Often, these questions become tied to worries about sexuality and gender identity. This only makes things more stressful! It's no wonder teen girls and young women dispro-portionately suffer from poor mental health. The good news is that Christianity, particularly confessional Lutheranism, has the tools to help you discern and express your authentic voice.

Before we can open the toolbox, let's take a side quest into the question of freedom. This might seem unrelated—but hang with me! Americans tend to understand freedom as negative. That obviously doesn't mean we think freedom is a bad thing. Americans love freedom as much as hotdogs and blowing things up. Rather, what it means is that Americans tend to assume freedom means being free from something, like being free from government interference in religious practice or speech. While this is a fine and important way of thinking about freedom, it's actually not how the great philosophers and theologians of the past conceptualized freedom. For them, freedom was positive, meaning we are free for something. More specifically, we are free to act according to our essence. The barriers that made it impossible for us to truly be ourselves are gone! This is how the New Testament authors write about our freedom in Christ.

Christ didn't die to set us free from the condemnation of the Law so that we could do whatever we want and go back to wallowing in sin. Rather, our freedom in the Gospel sets us free to serve our neighbor. We no longer have to worry about our own righteousness. Jesus sets us free for service to others. Moreover, your Baptism into Christ fully restores the image of God within you and conforms you to Christ so that you become what Martin Luther called "little Christs."

Now we can get back to the question of your voice. You are created in the image of God. The Triune God lovingly restores His image through Baptism into Christ by faith. Your true self is now conformed to Christ. You are a little Christ, free to act according to your essence. And what would Christ do? He serves us! As a baptized Christian, your true voice is Christ's voice, and you have been freed from sin, death, and the devil to use your voice in the service of your neighbor.

If your true voice is Christ's voice, does this destroy your unique personality or make your voice indistinguishable from your best friend's? Not at all! As the bride of Christ, our voice becomes more our own through our union with Him. Ideally, in a human marriage or even close platonic friendship, love and mutual self-sacrifice bring out your own unique voice more clearly. This is because mutual bonds of love remove the barriers of shame and self-consciousness that prevent us from being truly ourselves. Moreover, a self-sacrificing and loving husband or friend actively wants you to be yourself and speak your own voice. They are your greatest cheerleaders and bring your voice out of you.

Once your authentic and unique voice in Christ is clear, how should you exercise it? Do you say the same things to your parents and your friends? Probably not! So, you already know that we express ourselves differently in different circumstances. How we should use our voice and what exactly we should say depends on the context. As Lutherans, we might say that it depends on which "estate" we operate in and our vocation within that estate.

Early Lutheran theologians wrote about there being three "estates." These are the Church, the Home, and the State. After the Industrial Revolution in the early 1800s, many men began to work outside the home. Prior to the Industrial Revolution, most men and women worked together within the home. As a result, some modern theologians divided the estate of the Home into the Home and Economy. Additionally, Lutherans believe everyone has vocations, and not just those in professional church work like pastors or deaconesses. How do you get these vocations? God puts you there. You were born as a daughter and perhaps a sister and maybe a cousin. Later, you become a friend and maybe a wife. Perhaps you also become a mother and later an aunt or a grandmother. You are also a worker, whether you work outside the home or inside the home. You may be an employer, or you may be an employee. Right now, you are probably a student. Speaking of students, mine often worry about finding their "vocations" (by which they usually mean careers) or how to discern if they will choose a God-pleasing vocation. The good news is that as long as you are not participating in a sinful activity, your God-pleasing vocation is whatever you are doing at any given time. All vocations are good because God works through all of them as masks to provide for us. In this way, we serve others as little Christs.

In your vocations within the estate of the Home home (like daughter, sister, friend, wife, aunt, mother, etc.), we use our voices to build each other up and speak God's Word to one another. In the workplace, wherever it may be, you use your voice to serve your neighbor, be that the child you are homeschooling or the spreadsheet you are slaving over in an office cubicle.

In the estate of the Church, we are all members of the royal priesthood of all believers. As a royal priest, God wants you to use your voice to pray for others. Lutheran theologian John Kleinig writes about the importance of our priestly role as we bring others before God in prayer. All Christians should also use their voices to judge doctrine. That means reading your Bible and studying theology! You need to listen attentively to your pastor so that you can privately and respectfully correct him if he makes a public theological error. Your pastor wants you to use your voice this way. Even more amazingly, as royal priests, God tasks us—and you—with declaring the Gospel and the forgiveness of sins to repentant sinners. Who are these sinners? Most likely, they will be your family and friends. You use your voice to forgive others when they sin against you, but also to declare the forgiveness Christ won on the cross to your sisters in Christ when they confess their sins. Martin Luther talked about this great gift as the "mutual consolation of the saints." Use your voice to comfort others with the Gospel. You may also have a more specific vocation in the church, like serving as a baptismal sponsor, deaconess, cantor, or director of Christian education. Here, God also calls you to use your voice in the proclamation of the Law and Gospel.

Finally, after the Fall, we also live within the estate of the State. In the United States of America, we live in a democratic republic. This means you may exercise your voice by voting in public elections. You can also use your voice in the public political sphere by getting involved in activism for various causes or campaigns, such as the Pro-Life or Whole Life movements. You also exercise your voice by joining and participating in political parties.

But, sadly, that's not all. As you and I know all too well, the Old Eve clings to us even after Baptism. Our salvation is "now and not yet." We are already 100% saints, but we are simultaneously 100% sinners. Ouch. This means that we don't always do the good with our voices that we want to as baptized saints. I, for one, know this from plenty of experience. Running off at the mouth and saying impulsive and sometimes hurtful things is one of my besetting sins. So what to do? First, keep yourself in God's Word so you can recognize the sins you commit with your voice. Make sure you memorize the Ten Commandments! Run through them in your prayers each night to discern your sins. Did you gossip about your sister? Speak poorly of your parents? Say hateful things about a classmate? Repent!

And what if you don't recognize your sins? If you are blessed with Christian parents and other family members, try to listen when they say you've used your voice in a sinful way. Cultivate Christian friends who will tell you the truth about the things you say and the other ways you use your voice. The best friends make you a better person and lead you to Christ, and that includes sometimes saying hard things. Even harder is listening when our friends call us to repentance in this regard. Not too long ago, a new friend privately called me out for acting like a "bull in a china shop" on a social media group. And she was right! Although I hadn't seen it until then, I had been hurting others with the things I was saying, and I'm thankful she pointed it out.

The truth is that we all use our voices in sinful ways every day. We all sin in our vocations and against our neighbors. But God has Good News for you! God forgives you all your sins in Christ Jesus our Lord. Return to your Baptism daily and put on Christ's perfect righteousness with his perfectly pure voice. Read your Bible daily if possible and attend Divine Services every Sunday and Feast Day so you can hear the Word in the Absolution, Scripture readings, sermon, and hymns. Of course, you'll also have the opportunity to receive the very Word of God in His Body and Blood on your tongue and into your own body in the Lord's Supper. Finally, don't forget that as Lutherans, we have the great Gift of private confession and Absolution. Although the voice of Christ heard through the pastor is equally effective in forgiving sins on Sunday morning, you can derive great comfort from hearing the voice of the Good Shepherd forgive your particular personal sins through your pastor's vocal cords. The great Gift of Holy Absolution is that we actually hear the voice of Jesus from outside of us (no subjective inner voice in our minds), really forgiving our sins. Remember that your true identity and voice are "extrinsic." That means that after Baptism, they are found outside of you in Christ! God no longer hears the ways we've misused our voices. Instead, God only hears Christ's holy voice interceding for us in Heaven. Knowing that, we are free to use our voices to praise the Holy Trinity and serve others. Go, be free in Christ, and speak boldly!

# On Being Theologians

*Kelsi Klembara*

One of my recurrent fears is that I don't know enough. Every time I can't remember a fact or a Scripture reference, every time I listen to a recording of myself speaking (which I do somewhat frequently as a part of my job) and realize I didn't define a specific Christian doctrine precisely right, and every time I simply realize I'm just plain ignorant on a topic, this fear usually forms into some version of the following question:

"Am I qualified to think about and study God?"

You may or may not plan on pursuing theology as a vocation like me, but I wager that if you are a baptized Christian, you've had this thought at one time or another. Sadly, Christians often have the misconception that the study of God—theology proper—is reserved only for those called and ordained into the vocation of pastor. But this is neither a historically nor Scripturally accurate view of theology.

Martin Luther's emphasis on the priesthood of all believers revolutionized how normal, everyday Christian men and women viewed themselves, their relationship with God, and their relationships with each other. The medieval church had created a division between the spiritual roles of priest, nun, monk, etc., and temporal roles like mother, father, cobbler, farmer, and lawyer. Only the spiritually elite or spiritually enlightened could fulfill the former and, subsequently, gain access to God. In response to this, Luther and the other reformers emphasized justification by grace through faith in

Christ, pointing out how clearly Scripture proclaims that nothing we do makes us righteous, but instead, "Baptism, gospel, and faith alone make us spiritual and a Christian people."[1]

A key passage for this is Peter's description of the priesthood of all believers in which he states that in Christ, "you are a chosen race, a royal priesthood, a holy nation, a people for his own possession, that you may proclaim the excellencies of him who called you out of darkness into his marvelous light" (1 Peter 2:9).

Notice the progression here: Because we are chosen, we've been made into a royal priesthood so that we may proclaim and, therefore, know the Gospel. Our doing follows God's choosing. Our thinking about God follows our salvation in God.

Therefore, it is our righteousness in Christ, given through the authority of God's Word—not our vocation, our family, nor even our abilities and talents—that qualifies us for this priesthood. To be a baptized Christian is to be a part of the priesthood of all believers, and to be a part of the priesthood of all believers is to be a theologian. You and I are theologians! God has gifted us with a mind by which we can turn over His Words to us like a diamond with a radiance that never diminishes. We need our minds to digest His Word and hide it in our hearts (Psalm 119:10). We can and should use our rational capacities to "give an answer to everyone who asks you to give the reason for the hope that you have" (1 Peter 3:15). We are told:

> Whatever is true, whatever is honorable, whatever is just, whatever is pure, whatever is lovely, whatever is commendable, if there is any excellence, if there is anything worthy of praise, think about these things. What you have learned and received and heard and seen in me—practice these things, and the God of peace will be with you (Philippians 4:8-9, emphasis mine).

It's worth noting that all Christians, no matter their level of intellect or their vocational calling, are invited to engage with Scripture.

---

[1] Martin Luther, *Luther's Works, Vol. 44: The Christian in Society I*, ed. Jaroslav Jan Pelikan, Hilton C. Oswald, and Helmut T. Lehmann, vol. 44 (Philadelphia: Fortress Press, 1999), 127.

Called and ordained pastors are not privy to some special level of reason and intellect. God uses those qualified and called as shepherds of His church in order to ensure the proclamation of His Word and the administration of His sacraments.[2] The institution of this office provides order and unity for our body of believers (1 Peter 5) and guarantees that God's Gifts reach all sinner saints in need of forgiveness. For this, we can be grateful! But while pastors certainly receive special training in the study of Scripture and are necessary for its teaching and proclamation, this office does not forbid you, as a member of Christ's body, from cracking open your Bible, memorizing verses, asking questions, and learning from the Book of Life. "It is the duty of every Christian to espouse the cause of the faith, to understand and defend it, and to denounce every error,"[3] says Luther.

The clarity of Scripture further emboldens our individual claim as theologians. Also known as the perspicuity of Scripture, this is a basic tenant of the Reformation. God's Word is truth (John 17:17); it is God-breathed and meant for instruction, reproof, and training (2 Timothy 3:16). Scripture is light itself and therefore does not need to be illuminated (Psalm 119:105). This doesn't mean there are no difficult passages of Scripture by which we could all benefit from careful study and seeking wise counsel, but simply that Scripture is given to all of us. Its message is not hidden, and it does not require a special interpreter. God's Word is the very word of life (John 6:63)!

Thinking about and knowing God comes part and parcel with the Gift of faith in Christ. As a Gift, it is not meant to be measured or compared against that of your neighbor but instead to be enjoyed and to flow freely out of your faith in Christ. Perhaps this idea scares you. What does a theologian do, after all? What if you get it wrong? What if, like me, you are afraid of not knowing enough? Let me offer you a few descriptions that I hope will encourage you in your Christian freedom to delve into the depths of Scripture as a theologian—not

---

[2] See the Augsburg Confession Article V, "The Office of the Ministry," for a more detailed description of the pastoral office and how God uses this office to distribute his gifts.

[3] Martin Luther, *Luther's Works, Vol. 44: The Christian in Society I*, ed. Jaroslav Jan Pelikan, Hilton C. Oswald, and Helmut T. Lehmann, vol. 44 (Philadelphia: Fortress Press, 1999), 127.

because it makes you superior to anyone else nor gives you even an ounce of righteousness, but because you encouraged, sometimes even instructed, to use all of God's Gifts to live in relationship with Him, to enjoy Him and His goodness, and to be brought back again and again to the grace that is yours in Christ alone.

## So, what does a theologian do?

A theologian studies the Scriptures. Scripture is where God has chosen to reveal Himself and bestow to us His good Gifts. As Martin Luther says, Scripture is the cradle in which Christ is laid. Think of it this way: if Christ is the key by which you have access to all of God's Gifts, Scripture is the purse or bag in which that key is stored. The purse cannot unlock the door to God, but it's the only place you can find the key, and therefore, it serves an essential purpose.

We live in a time where there are so many tools to study Scripture: online podcasts and classes, Bible apps, digital theological libraries, audio playlists, and more are at our fingertips. Many of these are affordable or even free (like the resources at 1517.org). In addition to these, there are so many ways you can study Scripture! In group settings, on your own, at your church under the direction of your pastor, and with your family around the dinner table.

A theologian doesn't always get it right. Theologians are sinner saints in this life, which means we must continue to approach the authority of Scripture in humility, knowing we do what we do not want because of the sin within us (Romans 7:18-19). Even Peter, the theologian with the confession on which Christ establishes his church, made mistakes—and big ones at that! Remember when he went around asserting that Christians had to be circumcised? (Galatians 2) We all have our blind spots. Humility—and a willingness to be corrected—is key when we approach Scripture. This is made so much easier when we let that first confession made by Peter, "You are the Messiah, the Son of the living God," guide and direct us (Matthew 16:16). This confession guides and protects us when we seek answers, repent of misunderstandings, and continue to proclaim the truth that is given to us.

A theologian submits themselves to wise counsel. It's exactly because of the above that theologians submit themselves to the authority of wise teachers and leaders. This should be the pastor of your church because part of their official role as God's mouthpiece is to answer your questions, divvy out Absolution to your confessions, and guide you in Scripture. But this can also be found in older Christians you trust– their job as theologians is to teach you, advise you, and mentor you (Titus 2). Don't be afraid to give someone this responsibility that otherwise has yet to claim it! I'm serious: ask an older and wiser woman in your congregation to get coffee, get to know them, and tell them you want to learn from them or alongside them. They may not feel qualified, but I guarantee they will be honored.

A theologian lets Scripture breathe. As I've already written, our reason is a Gift from God, yet reason has its limits. We submit our reason to the authority of Scripture, and where Scripture doesn't speak, neither do we. We let the plain and clear text of Scripture proclaim what God has chosen to reveal to us in Law and Gospel. This can be a more difficult task than you would think because we humans love to tie everything up in a neat bow. We want all of our why questions answered, but unfortunately, the task of the theologian is to proclaim only what has been revealed to us in Scripture, namely Christ himself.

A theologian centers on Christ and the cross. All knowledge of the Bible, of Scripture, and of God must be viewed in light of the person and work of Jesus Christ. This is not just the first confession but the last one as well. Christ has lived, Christ is risen, and Christ will come again. Christ is the object of our faith. He is the final pursuit of our knowledge and the foundation of truth itself. St. Paul said it best, "For I decided to know nothing among you except Jesus Christ and him crucified" (1 Corinthians 2:2).

Are you qualified to be a theologian? No matter your vocation, your age, your sex, or your qualification, as a baptized Christian, you most certainly are. God wants you to think about Him and to know Him. He has gifted you with a sound mind to be curious about Him, to ask questions when you don't know, and to assert truth claims about who He is and who you are in Him, however imperfectly. He's not mad when you get things wrong; He's not bothered if you can't remember what you learned last week. He is a living and breathing God—a person, three in one, who delights that you know Him because He has claimed you as His own.

# On Respect

*Deaconess Raquel Rojas*

Dear Sisters in Christ,

"Respect" is a word that is used by a lot of people in various circumstances. Sometimes, people use the word to mean due regard for people's thoughts, feelings, traditions, and perspectives. Other times, people use the word for giving particular honor or deference to those in particular positions. It is true, too, that the word can be misused as people think that they should demand respect from others or that they deserve it out of a sense of entitlement.

A lot could be written about "respect" for Christians. As I have thought and prayed about this, I have noted these seven areas that deal with respect that have helped me as I have navigated life as a woman, a daughter, a sister, a friend, and a deaconess. Perhaps they can be helpful for you as you navigate "respect" in your own life and as you grow as a child of God.

## 1. The Lord's Respect toward Us

We may not think of the Lord respecting us. Yet, in His Word, we learn that He rejoices over us with singing (Zephaniah 3:17). He loves us with an everlasting love and continues His faithfulness to us (Jeremiah 31:3). He fearfully and wonderfully made us (Psalm 139:14). "I have redeemed you. I have called you by name. You are mine," He declares (Isaiah 43:1).

When He made us, He created us with free will, allowing us to forsake Him. That means that we can choose to disrespect Him. He demonstrates with this that we are not puppets whose strings are pulled or computers that are programmed to like Him and do every single thing He says. With respect for His creation, He gives us the ability to reject His promises. He does this to demonstrate extravagant grace to us, regardless of how we respond to Him.

In Genesis 3, we learn how He allows us to make choices that are harmful to us. Adam and Eve, our parents in Paradise, did exactly that. And yet, even there, He offered a promise that the enemy one day would be defeated (Genesis 3:15). He guides us by His Spirit working through the Word even when we fail to heed His advice and counsel. We can be grateful that He sent His Son Jesus to save us from sin and death and to be the Way, the Truth, and the Life for us. The Gifts of His work are given to us through His Word and Sacraments.

And yet, this does not allow us to do whatever we want with our bodies. In 1 Corinthians 6, we learn that we are called to glorify God with our bodies. In today's world, people often believe that respect for themselves and their bodies allows them to make any kind of decisions they want with their bodies. That is not what Jesus teaches us. The respect that the Lord has for us does not allow us to do whatever we want with our bodies. We are baptized into Christ to live each day, taking care of our bodies by eating correctly, exercising, sleeping, working, and having adequate time for refreshment. It also means that we are not our own and we have been bought with a price.

## 2. The Lord's Respect for His Law

The Lord respects His Law and insists that it be followed. Unlike others in the world who frequently disregard the law of the land, the Lord has established His Law and desires it to be followed. He respects it so much that He does not make exceptions. There are no loopholes. Thankfully, this is why He sent His Son Jesus to fulfill the Law perfectly for us. In the great exchange, Jesus gives us His righteousness as He takes our sins away. The wages of sin is death but the free gift of God is eternal life through Jesus Christ (Romans 6:23).

Even though we cannot fulfill the Law because of our sin, the Law is good. It is good that we have the Law. We can be thankful for the Lord's standards and for His design for us. We also can be grateful that He does not haphazardly change things, but He remains solid, faithful, and true in a world that often is the opposite.

## 3. The Lord's Call for Us to Respect Him

The Lord calls us to respect Him. He indicates this in many places, especially in the First, Second, and Third Commandments. We are not to have any other gods, nor are we to misuse His Name but call upon His Name as He has given it to us and hear and learn His Holy Word. Take some time to recall the meanings of those Commandments in Luther's Small Catechism. Nobody else is in the same place as the Lord (First Commandment). Only He gets the respect that is afforded in prayer, praise, and thanksgiving (Second Commandment). His Word is that which we are called to hear and learn gladly as we respect the Word by regarding it to be sacred (Third Commandment).

## 4. Respect as Something We Give

As the Lord has loved us, so we are to love one another (John 13:34-35). Just as we have received respect and are called to respect God's Word, respect is something that we give appropriately. The Fourth Commandment and its meaning in Luther's Small Catechism are helpful to remember. Respect is something we give to those in authority over us, including our parents, grandparents, instructors, and the like. We offer it in response to God's grace and because of the Lord making us His holy people.

Another thing to remember is that it does not depend on whether we like the people in authority over us. Time and again, we have people in authority who disappoint us, lie to us, belittle us, and bring other harm to us. We may not vote for them or support their policies. And yet, we are called to pray for them as we respect them, giving them appropriate honor as they are called to lead without groaning or complaining (Hebrews 13:17). This is not easy to do, but that is another reason why receiving the Word and Sacraments regularly is so important.

## 5. Respect as a Gift Received

People often think they deserve respect when, in reality, it is often earned. We do not live in order to be respected; we respect others by the way we live, in humility to God and in submission and reverence to Him.

This can be seen as a big surprise. In today's world, the notion of "entitlement" makes people believe that they deserve certain things. People include "respect" on the list of things they think they always deserve. Even if we should be respected due to our vocations in life, we do not live for that respect. We do not serve in order to be respected. Instead, like Christ, we serve and love even when we are persecuted and disrespected (Matthew 5:43-44). We even do this when people we mentor or for whom we care about ignore us, slander us, or berate us. We realize that their rejection of us gives us a glimpse of how we reject the Lord. And even when we are not respected as perhaps we should be, we remain kind, tenderhearted, and forgiving (Ephesians 4:32) since we love and serve even when we are disrespected. Interestingly, others may see our light shining in this way and give glory, honor, and praise to our Father in heaven (Matthew 5:14-16).

## 6. Respect and Worship

As you might have noticed, the ability to respect and worship are closely related. We receive Gifts in worship that empower us to offer respect to God and to others around us. We learn in worship of God's respect for His creation and His Law. We also experience in worship the amazing nature of the Lord's heart and grow in our gratefulness for being baptized into Christ.

With that, then, we participate in the life of the Church as members of His Body. We recognize that our value is not in "making ourselves up" but in the dignity of whom our Lord has made us. With awe and reverence, our dress and our manner of life reflect all those wholesome virtues with which the Lord has gifted us. Every day of our lives, then, offers us an opportunity to worship the Lord by respecting those around us, not living for the respect of others, and serving just as Christ served, even when we may not receive the respect we wish.

## 7. Ways We Respect Each Other

Our respect for God, driven by the Holy Spirit, becomes the springboard from which we respect each other. Only by His Spirit do we receive the strength to offer respect to other people. That is why it is so important to meditate daily on the Word of God and to be present with other believers in the Divine Service. Receiving the Lord's Gifts, we are given the gifts that help us to offer respect to other people around us.

Kind words written or texted, grace-filled responses to those around us, listening ears to those who speak, and an ongoing trust in God are just some of the ways we can respect those around us. We pray for each other, and we direct all people to the One who deserves all our honor, praise, and respect: Jesus Christ.

I hope these are helpful for you as you grow in respect for the Lord, His Word, and His people.

Grace, mercy, and peace,
Deaconess Raquel A. Rojas

# On Work

*Katie Chester*

From an early age, we are taught to dream and to have goals for the direction of our lives. Our teachers, coaches, and family encouraged us to pursue these dreams. What college will you attend? What degree will you pursue? Careers were decided, and colleges were selected. Some of us dreamed of joining the workforce—launching a career and making a difference. Others dreamed of becoming mothers, tending to their children with their undivided attention. We were motivated by what would be given to us in the pursuit of our own self-interest. If you are reading this, it is most likely because your dream did not turn into the reality you expected (along with most of us!).

I'll tell you about my career journey—one of struggle, growth, and perseverance—beginning at 19 years old. I recall confidently declaring to my parents that I would never get married and never have children. I'd be traveling the world, reading, and writing poetry. The next day, I met the love of my life (at a Higher Things conference, no less). I told him I would certainly never be a pastor's wife. In the blink of an eye—marriage, two babies, and five years passed. In 2020, my husband broached the topic, "I think God is calling me to Seminary." That night, I could feel God chuckling at me for the declaration I made five years prior.

God opened door after door for us to pursue this life change. My husband and I left our comfortable careers and our families and moved cross-country. Suddenly, life was different. Our baby boys were in daycare for the first time and were no longer cared for by relatives. My husband began school, and I started a new career in tech, which I began to love. Becoming the sole income source for our family was certainly a shift, but it was a decision we made together, fully aware of the sacrifices we would be making. It was the biggest exercise in faith and trust that I'd ever experienced.

"Trust in the Lord with all your heart, and do not lean on your own understanding,
     In all your ways acknowledge him, and he will make straight your paths." Proverbs 3:5-6

As a working wife providing for my family, including my husband and children, I faced some judgment and condescension from people who thought there was only one way to provide and one person who could provide... the husband. I was used to the occasional raised eyebrow or underhanded comment, being a female manager in technology in a male-dominated company. To feel judged by other Christians for simply stepping up and taking care of my family was hurtful. The root of the judgment stemmed from me simply being the person providing for my family at a time when it was both needed and required of me. It was certainly not borne out of selfish intent.

Comparison crept in quickly, causing me to feel envious of women who were able to stay home with their children because of the judgment I received. I struggled with the perception of being a selfish mother who was happy in her career at the expense of her children. As I untangled the web of emotions, I connected with other working mothers and women to see if I was alone. These women—friends, colleagues, acquaintances—shared their experiences, encouragements, grievances, and cautions. Most had reasons for working that aligned with mine and had similar feelings of comparisons and missing out. Their advice varied from a healthy pushback on balancing motherhood and a career to advocating for swift career growth when possible.

I began to understand that the feelings I felt were not unique to Christians but to most working mothers and women. As I came to this realization, I didn't understand the biblical reasons being referenced that would suggest there would be issues with the concept of the wife working, even if I were choosing to work while my husband also had a career.

## Spoiler: There are none!

> "Do nothing from selfish ambition or conceit, but in humility count others more significant than yourselves. Let each of you look not only to his own interests, but also to the interests of others." Philippians 2:3–4

The concept of working as a wife and as a mother is not sinful. When you choose to set aside the vocations that Christ has blessed you with, wife, mother, or both, and focus on working for selfish gain, it can become sinful. Do you go to work for vain reasons—self-interest, rank, an escape? Or do you work to use your gifts to serve others and serve your family? Sin fills our lives daily, but the intent of working is rarely, if at all, an outcome of a sinful decision.

> "She seeks wool and flax, And works with willing hands, She is like the ships of the merchant; She brings her food from afar. She rises when it is yet night, And provides food for her household and portions for her maidens. She considers a field and buys it; out of her earnings she plants a vineyard. She sets about her work vigorously; her arms are strong for her tasks. She sees that her trading is profitable, and her lamp does not go out at night." Proverbs 31:13-18

Proverbs 31 is an encouragement. That lovely Proverbs 31 woman had the confidence in herself and in her work to purchase fields, trade goods, and had the strength to serve her family with her work. Her husband had trust in her to carry out all her work, so much so that he praised her for it!

You might find yourself working because it is essential during this season of life. It's not an easy choice, but you know that you are supporting your family. This is not sinful.

You might be career-driven, focused on using your gifts to the best of your ability in the workplace. Seeing the impact of your work brings you joy and fulfillment. This is not sinful.

You might be a stay-at-home mom who misses the professional workplace. You miss your coworkers and adult interaction, and you miss learning and growing. These feelings can lead to shame and guilt, making you hesitant to change your mind. This is not sinful.

Do any of these resonate with you? My friend, know that you are not alone. Balancing work, life, family, and every other stressor is a heavy burden. You are doing an incredible job, and I empathize with you.

Working isn't sinful. Neither is staying at home to be a parent. But we do manage to sin while doing both of them. There is no way to stay at home and be a mom without being a sinner. There is no way to work without being a sinner. "Wherever you go, you bring yourself with you." It applies beautifully to this scenario. We cannot run from our innate sinful nature. No matter which path we choose, working or not, we are still sinners. There is no way to live, to work in a vocation, without sinning.

Jesus does not love women who stay home for their families any more than those who have careers. He does not love you less because that meeting ran over, and you missed another family dinner. He sees your efforts, your love, and your heart. He sees your failures, your doubt, and your guilt as a woman, a wife, and mother. He sees you for who you are, His baptized daughter, who He died and rose for. Your worth as a woman cannot be tied up in your decisions to be a stay-at-home mom or wife or work outside the home. Your worth as a woman is secure in Christ, your Savior.

Place your faith at the top of your priorities. As working women, we often have busy schedules, and our faith can unintentionally take a backseat. Fill your cup up first! Set time aside to pray, meditate, and read God's Word. Stay grounded in your faith and use this in your work. These quiet moments of reflection will bring you peace through the chaos.

Lean into your talents. God richly blesses us with spiritual Gifts. When your work is aligned with your spiritual Gifts, life becomes richer, simpler. It is the intersection of the secular aspect of your life with your faith—something so beautiful and rare to behold in today's life. You might not know your gifts now, but you will come to understand them as you try different vocations. Some gifts include leadership, mercy, administration, service, and teaching. As an example, those with the gift of administration find enjoyment in creating organization and efficiency. Those with the gift of leadership naturally take charge of situations with ease. Finding an occupation where you can serve your neighbor with your gifts is truly transformative.

Show up to work with your full self; do not diminish the parts of you that you love or make yourself smaller for others. Let Christ's light shine through in everything you do; exemplify kindness, humility, and integrity. Keep showing up with that joy and positivity. Turn the other cheek to gossip and speak well of others. Let your work be done in love. On the hard days, the following verse was written on a worn-out Post-it note stuck to my computer monitor. It reminded me to find the positive in situations.

> "Finally, brothers, whatever is true, whatever is honorable, whatever is just, whatever is pure, whatever is lovely, whatever is commendable, if there is any excellence, if there is anything worthy of praise, think about these things." Philippians 4:8

Friend, I leave you with this. As a woman in the workforce, I encourage you to remember your strengths, gifts, and, most importantly, dreams. You have freedom in Christ to consider how to use your gifts and how to serve others. I hope you feel empowered to make these decisions. Had I let the peer pressure and fear of judgment determine my path, I would not be pursuing my dreams right alongside my husband who is pursuing his own. How beautiful Christ's guidance and path for our lives! Rely on Him; place your trust in Him. Rest in the comfort of knowing He loves you and does not look down on you for your work. With this, I hope you bring the light of Christ with you in all that you do!

# On Teaching

*Katherine Swem*

Have you ever considered that your whole life has been spent learning? Even before birth, you learned about the world from the shelter of your mother's womb. Over time, learning became more formal for you at home or at school. As you reflect on your God-given Gifts and possible future vocations, perhaps you might consider helping others and sharing the wisdom you have received.

Maybe God blessed you with a teacher who opened your eyes to the understanding and love of a particular subject, and you hope to do the same for others. Or you were given the Gift of a teacher who understood and encouraged you right when you had a great need. Or perhaps, recognizing the snares and temptations of the world, you would love a vocation inside the ark of the Church.

St. Paul writes in Colossians 3:16, "Let the word of Christ dwell in you richly, teaching and admonishing one another in all wisdom, singing psalms and hymns and spiritual songs, with thankfulness in your heart to God." This teaching, admonishing, and singing is woven into the school day in Lutheran schools, and it is such a blessing for students and teachers alike. St. Paul continues, "And, whatever you do, in word or deed, do everything in the name of the Lord Jesus, giving thanks to God the Father through him." For the Lutheran teacher, theology is not simply a class taught at a certain time of the day. Rather, the beauty and order of the Father's creation and the saving love of Christ permeate every subject and interaction. The classroom can be a place of true thankfulness for all the Gifts God lavishes upon us.

To talk about teaching is really to talk about parents and children. God willing, it was due to the love and faithfulness of your parents that you were brought to the waters of Holy Baptism. As a small child, you had much to learn about the wonders of God's creation and of His promise of salvation for all people—for you. In His faithfulness to every generation, God provides parents who are tasked with an immense honor and responsibility. Proverbs 22:6 tells us, "Train up a child in the way he should go; even when he is old he will not depart from it." Trusting and relying on God, Christian parents faithfully take on this task with joy.

God blessed me with two Lutheran teachers as parents. My mom laid aside classroom teaching to pour out her love of holy Scripture, hymnody, art, literature, and nature on her children. She made learning a beautiful adventure, and I wanted to be just like her. Meanwhile, my dad, a Lutheran teacher and church musician, went off to school each day, and I couldn't wait to go, too.

In time, I found such joy in being a student in the classroom. (Maybe you share that joy, too.) I loved my teachers, and I watched them. I soaked up knowledge and delighted in opportunities for creativity. I looked forward to the day when I would have my dear dad as my teacher, and due to changing needs at the school, he taught me for several years throughout my education.

Having my dad as my teacher for years on end could have been a burden, but he was a teacher who achieved a type of magic. His classroom was simple and orderly. He had high expectations for his students, held their respect, and managed behavior with a word or his patented "look of death." We were assured we would be cared for and were expected to care for each other. He brought rich content to our classes and taught us to delight in what was true. He understood that great storytelling draws the learner close, and in this way, he captivated us with Dickens, American History, and the lives of the saints and martyrs. We were held to a high standard of work and expression while enjoying his wit, humor, and genuine love of each student. In every subject and throughout classroom life, he taught us the promises of God and the surety of our salvation. I wanted to be a teacher like my dad, too.

At school and home, I was blessed by parents who had been given the Gift of teaching. When parents choose to send their children to a Lutheran school, the teacher stands in loco parentis, "in the place of a parent," taking their authority from the Fourth Commandment. What an honor to stand in that place. Teaching beloved, Baptized children about the Father who created them, the Son who redeemed them, and the Holy Spirit who sanctified them is certainly a responsibility and blessed vocation!

I came to teaching through the influence of my parents and other beloved teachers. In doing so, I became a link in a lengthy chain of those desiring to pass on the Christian faith, the wonder of the created world, skills needed to flourish, and virtues for living in love with one another.

Have you been inspired by those who guided you in learning? Do you wonder what it takes to teach in a Lutheran school? Teaching requires a desire to learn and grow continually. You must know and love the learners placed into your classroom by God. Teachers must work toward excellence in intellectual training while serving the very practical (and sometimes messy) needs of others. Chiefly, a Lutheran teacher must be fed with God's Word and Sacraments, continually being strengthened to bring wisdom and the mercy of our Savior into every aspect of classroom life. This is a beautiful and challenging task.

Blessings abound in the freedom of teaching in Lutheran schools. I am blessed to serve at a school that begins each day with Morning Prayer or Matins led by our pastor. The preaching of God's Word, praying, singing, and reciting the Scriptures and Catechism shape our school day and culture. In our classes, we study and discuss God's Word, giving thanks to God in times of blessing, praying for His mercy in trouble, and continuing to sing hymns and recite God's Word throughout our day. What a gift to these young, baptized souls! What a gift to me!

In a world that is continually confused, we teach and confess the Truth. Standing on the solid foundation of Christ, we are free to explore First Article wonders around us, always seeing the world as it is—created, redeemed, and sanctified by our loving God. I'm thankful to teach at a classical Lutheran school that provides an excellent curriculum focusing on goodness, truth, and beauty. I am free to expand out from this curriculum without the rigidity faced in many schools. Offering students embodied experiences that weave together knowledge across the curriculum brings delight. Studying plant life in science means heading out to the woods to greet and identify emerging spring wildflowers. Reading *Meet Paddington* includes making Paddington's recipe for orange marmalade and dressing up for a British tea. Coming across questions on the End Times in theology prompts a visit from our pastor for a knowledgeable and comforting discussion. At a Lutheran school, I am free to use time and resources to benefit my students in individual and personal ways.

As Lutheran teachers, the troubles caused by sin are approached far differently than in the world. When we live close together—students, teachers, administrators, parents, congregation members, pastors—the Body of Christ continually faces the heartbreak of sinning against one another. In Lutheran classrooms, the Law shows where the conscience has gone astray. Students confess and repent, offering and receiving Christ's forgiveness, sharing the sweet and life-giving words of the Gospel. This use of Law and Gospel and its pattern of forgiveness bear fruit in our schools, churches, and in the world. What a blessing to teach children the utter relief, freedom, and joy found in God's grace.

Teaching, like all vocations, is also marked with crosses. To teach well, continual, hard work is required. This can lead the teacher to pride (and over-working) or despair (leaving work undone). Teaching with peaceful diligence is only possible through the work of the Holy Spirit. Standing in loco parentis is challenging when all parents, teachers, and students working together are sinners in constant need of God's grace. Students are continually waging war against temptation, facing challenges in mind and body, and experiencing difficult circumstances in and out of school. As their leader, it is easy to feel burdened, ill-equipped, and weary while trying to impart wisdom and goodness.

Thanks be to God that he does not abandon his children. The work is God's work. He uses my hands in His service to my young neighbors, forgives my many failures, and provides me with wisdom, strength, and peace to accomplish His good and gracious will. If you enter this beautiful vocation, He will forgive, protect, and provide for you, too. Nourishment for our souls is constantly being given in His Holy Word (look especially to the Psalms), and guidance and encouragement come from dear pastors, headmasters, mentor teachers, and our own parents.

All in all, for those who have been given the Gift of teaching, there is daily and continual joy. Like a child's parents, teachers witness the miracle of a growing child. Children make dramatic leaps and bounds in stature, knowledge, and faith in Christ in the course of a school year, and every day, their teacher is given the honor of observing, forming, encouraging, and celebrating that growth.

Amazingly, at the end of a class period, at the end of the day, at the end of the year, all of this effort is not simply temporal. While time with dear baptized souls passes quickly, we have the assurance our joy will be complete for all time together in heaven with Jesus.

# On Music

## Lisa Clark

This is what I can remember: It was a warm Sunday after the morning services. It was probably Holy Week (so Palm Sunday), and it was probably 2008. I was in the car with our kids, and my husband (a pastor) had to run back into the church to grab something he had forgotten. Chances were, he'd talk to a few more folks on his way back out.

My mind wandered back to the Holy Weeks of my high school years when my then-crush-now-husband was Pontius Pilate in what our church called the Passion Play. I was Council Member #2. The annual event, presented primarily by the youth, integrated all four Gospels to provide a dramatized version of Holy Thursday and Good Friday. Council Member #1 had the best line of the whole script: "His blood be on us and our children," taken from Matthew 27:25.

As a teenager, that line always gave me chills. At age 25, it still did. As I sat in the car, I thought to myself, "Someone really needs to write a hymn on that line." A moment later, I thought, "I wonder if I could." I had never written a hymn before (This is actually not true, as I'll share later). Even though we had a very new hymnal (shoutout to Lutheran Service Book), I had not given much thought to how new hymns were written. But I had written poetry, including sonnets, in college. It occurred to me that an Elizabethan sonnet had three quatrains (stanzas?) and a couplet (refrain?), so I found a piece of paper in the car and decided to give it a try.

My husband came back and was thrilled to know a new hymn had just been written. We realized that this meter would work with the tune *Finlandia*, and he could not have been more encouraging about my writing repertoire which now included hymn texts. Both pastors of the congregation asked me to write texts on occasion, and I wrote others for fun. Through various interactions, editors of Concordia Publishing House's music department encouraged me as well.

About five years and two dozen hymns later, I marveled at how God led me to people, opportunities, and training that encouraged me in my writing and challenged me to hone my skills. By that time, a few of my hymns had been published, but it would still be a few years before that first text received a meter makeover, a tune by Mark Knickelbein, and a publication as a choral piece entitled "The Blood of Jesus." Even so, I had been encouraged by numerous pastors, composers, and musicologists to keep writing. It was a bit of a jolt, then, when I was met one day with this comment by another Lutheran woman: "Oh. I didn't think women could write hymns." Can we?

Dear sister in Christ, you may have been wondering why I spent the first part of my letter to you as a biographical narrative. You may also be wondering why I decided to share this incident in 2013. I want you to know, friend, that if God equips you with the gifts, training, and encouragement needed to write hymn texts, you may face a similar story. I want you to know that you're not alone, and I want to share how I worked through this important consideration.

I mentioned a moment ago that I had not always thought about the origins of hymns. As I began writing a few, I realized that only a few people look at the fine print at the bottom of a hymn to see who wrote the text or tune. At the time, this seemed like a relatively inconspicuous way for me to serve my brothers and sisters in Christ. Even so, I subconsciously knew early on that our hymnal included hymns written by pastors and non-pastors, by men and women, by Lutherans and non-Lutherans. Despite this knowledge, I wanted to take this question very seriously. Even though plenty of pastors and church leaders were already encouraging me to write, I wanted to take a moment and reassure myself that this was indeed a faithful and God-pleasing vocation.

I could have gone straight to LSB and counted how many women's names were in the indexes of contributors (about forty women and a hundred hymns, accounting for about one in five hymns). I could have recalled that Martin Luther knew Elisabeth Cruciger, a Reformation-era hymnist, and likely encouraged her work. But like any typical Lutheran, I started with the Bible. Was there any warning against women writing hymns? Were there any examples of women singing original sacred songs in the Bible?

Dear sister, you know this answer. You know that one of the most beloved songs from the Bible comes from Mary, the mother of Jesus, who sang what we now call the Magnificat. But did you know that she wasn't alone? Miriam, Deborah, Hannah, Elizabeth, and others are recorded as having sung (and likely "written") original songs. In fact, it seems that when the Bible records the words of women regarding God, those words are most often in song. (But let's not forget Deborah—again, Ruth, Abigail, and others who shared their faith in conversations and the like.)

It encouraged me that God saw fit to include women in the Church's song even within His Holy Word. It encourages me as I continue studying many hymnists and learning of other women who serve(d) in this vocation. It encourages me when I recall the kind messages that so many leaders from our church body have shared with me to continue in this work.

If you, too, think that God may be leading you to consider the role of a hymnist, here is my own letter of encouragement to you.

You don't need much to get started. Years after my scrap-paper-in-the-car draft, I remembered that I had written two other hymns prior to that. One was in second grade. My teacher read us a devotion that encouraged us to write a song about Jesus to a tune we knew. I did and handed it to my teacher later that day. She complimented me on my effort and handed it back. I'm terrible at throwing things away, but I'm sure that first little hymn is nowhere to be found. My second hymn was in high school. My music theory exercise was to try writing a melody. I started with the text. If we ever meet in person, ask me about that humorous disaster! The point is that all three of my first attempts were simple drafts written without much guidance.

To get beyond those first drafts, however, you need an army. Don't worry; it can be a small one. Gather for yourself a couple of people who are steeped in the Bible, a few who are terrific at writing, a few who will be very kind, and a few who will be very honest. You can assign some people to double duty. At some point, you'll also want to find a few who are terrific at composing music. Fun fact: It's pretty rare for someone to be equally good at texts and tunes. I love that collaboration is practically required for a hymn to come together.

You already know this, but you absolutely need the Bible. You also need a hymnal. Read the Bible all the time so the Word lives within you, and so you have references, allusions, and themes as part of your natural writing language. Read the hymnal, too. Study the rhyme and meter of your favorite hymns. Notice turns of phrases that stand out to you. Think about how one stanza leads to the next within the flow of a hymn text. There are certainly books that talk about hymns but start with your primary sources. No doubt, Luther's Small Catechism will help too.

As with all things, surround your work in prayer. Dear sister, if your hymn text is ever sung, people will be singing your words of faith as if they are their own. This is no small thing! To quote our fellow sister hymnist Mary, "Behold, I am the servant of the Lord" (Luke 1:38). Pray for guidance to write faithfully and well, neither falling into pride nor despair because it is God who prepares work for you to do, including your writing.

I already mentioned that I love the collaborative nature that hymnody requires. Think about it. A hymnist needs to write the text. A composer needs to write the tune. Congregational leaders need to plan it into a service. Musicians need to practice and lead. Singers need to sing. What a beautiful demonstration of the body of Christ working together in praising God! Even if you read this entire letter knowing that you may not ever write words to a hymn, I pray that this letter blesses you as you consider the many ways that God uses you. Maybe you write tunes, play music, or sing along. Regardless, it's a joy to partner with you as a fellow sister in Christ, united in faith and song.

# On Mental Health

*Deaconess Emma Heinz*

Before He died, Jesus, quoting Psalm 22, cried, "My God, my God, why hast thou forsaken me?" Jesus asked why the omnipresent, omnipotent, omniscient Lord of all had left Him to suffer and die a sinner's death—a death Jesus did not deserve. On the outside looking in, the supposed anointed one of God hung, rejected by the very God of Whom Jesus claimed to be begotten. How can God's chosen one be left hung out to dry? How can the Son of God, claimed by His Father at His Baptism, now endure suffering in groanings too deep for words? How can God allow such things? We know how Jesus' crucifixion ends: in His death and subsequent resurrection. But what about you and me? What happens when it's all too much - the pain, the suffering, the depression, the despair?

Mental health and mental illness come up in conversation more and more in the church. As the Church wrestles with her response to mental health and mental illness, Christians struggling with poor mental health often find themselves left without help, understanding, or comfort. If this is you, dear sister, know that the Lord sees you and knows you. I want you also to know you have sisters in Christ with whom to share your burdens, tears, and hurt.

Mental illness is not new, and it hasn't always been well understood. Every era of history has brought a new name for "chronic brain funk." What we now call depression has also been described as melancholy, spiritual attack, or female hysteria. Whatever its name, the concept of your mind turning against you and driving you into despair and isolation remains a constant and abiding thorn. The mind, a great gift of God, is not untouched by sin. When our minds betray us, we are left lost and afraid. The mind, with its God-given ability to create, love, learn, and problem-solve, which before the Fall into sin praised the Maker of all without fail, is now corrupted and broken by sin. In some cases, Satan attacks us through our frail and failing minds, feeding us thoughts that seek to destroy from the inside out. In the worst of cases, Satan's lies can lead a person to question whether being alive is even worth the trouble. It is not an easy thing to struggle with mental illness. For something that might be "all in your head," there are very real and lasting effects.

So what do we do about it? We know that mental illness is complicated. Its causes are still not widely known, even while extensively studied. The effects of mental illness range from mild inconveniences, like bad days or occasional bouts of tears, to total disruption of your everyday life. What is normally easy, like eating, taking care of yourself and others, engaging with God's Word, and receiving His Gifts, are now difficult, if not impossible, all because your mind cannot climb out of whatever pit you find yourself in. Like any problem, we try to solve it. We try to alleviate the suffering we see and experience. We try to understand why mental illness happens and how it affects us. We try to understand what is happening to us and in us so that we can exert control over the situation. If I become the master of my mind, it can't turn against me. If you have enough power, mental illness can't break you. It's a series of "if, then" statements that only offer limited relief at best and delusion at worst. Thanks be to God that our Lord does not leave us to fumble our way to and through failing comforts.

God gives words to the suffering, downtrodden, and despairing. He gives us words to speak back to Him, with voices filled with anger, sadness, frustration, and hopelessness. From the depths of woe, from the valley of the shadow of death, from the grave, we call out to our God. Our God is not far away, sheltering Himself from the horrors of a world ravaged by sin, death, and the devil. Our God is near, nearer even than we know. We do not have a God that shies away from the suffering, the broken, the sick, the weak, and the helpless.

Our God, in His infinite wisdom, created the world and her inhabitants, knowing mankind would be the undoing of the perfect "very good" goodness in the Garden of Eden. He created all things, spoke them into being, formed them from the ground, and breathed life into man and woman, knowing they would sin. They sought to be God and, in so doing, damned the whole world. They broke everything. They could no longer be with God. They were cast out of the garden, cursed to suffer because of sin, cursed to die because death had entered the world, and cursed to eternal separation from their God. But God did not abandon His children. He didn't demand that Adam and Eve work to fix the problem they created. He knew they would never be able to.

Instead, God promised the Messiah, the Savior, the eternal fix for the mess in which Adam and Eve now lived. God reminded humanity of this promise throughout the Old Testament. He selected Israel to be His chosen people, not because of their adherence to His laws, but because of His love for His creation. When the Savior finally came, the Word of God, the Second Person of the Trinity, Who had been since eternity, took on a finite, frail form—the feeble frame of a man. Immanuel—God with us. This eternal God-Man is Jesus, Who is the Christ. This Jesus, who lived a human life full of suffering and joy alike, was crucified, died, and was buried. Dead. And then, in the greatest miracle of all, Jesus rose from the dead, bursting the bonds of death, undoing the stain of sin, and sucker-punching Satan in the face. God knows we cannot free ourselves from sin, so He stepped in to save us. He knows the struggles we face daily.

I don't know why God allows us to suffer in this way, with thoughts that drive us away from Him. What I do know is this: You are baptized into the death and resurrection of Christ Jesus, your Lord, Who came to you, a condemned, lost, dead sinner, and brought you to life everlasting. You are given salvation through Jesus. You have this promise in the waters of Baptism, where water and word combine to make you God's child. Water, even a daily shower, can remind you constantly of who and Whose you are. You are given food for the fight in the Body and Blood of Jesus, in, with, and under the bread and wine at the Lord's Table. The invitation to this feast is given to all who believe in the forgiveness of sins. You are a child of God. You are an heir of the Kingdom of God. Call on your Heavenly Father for aid, as any beloved child runs to their father for comfort. You are now a part of the Body of Christ, His Church. When one part suffers, the whole body feels it and surrounds the hurting member with love, and care, and rest.

What I do know is this: You are not so broken that God, the Maker and Redeemer of all, won't care for you. You aren't alone in this world, even when your thoughts lead you to see only your worries, anxieties, needs, and fears, and not the people in your life given to love you.

What I do know is this: At the Last Day, God will wipe away all tears from your eyes. You will see the face of God, not because you deserve to but because of the sacrificial love of God. The love that created the world, knowing it would be broken, the love that sent forth the Savior to fix the brokenness, the love that sustains you even amidst the suffering you still endure.

It is entirely possible, dear sister, that the mental health struggles you endure here and now will not go away. I pray they do. I pray that God, in His mercy, takes away these burdens. I pray you never experience thoughts of depression and despair in the first place. But in the event that these thoughts do not recede permanently or even for a time, take comfort in knowing God sees you. God the Father, having created you and made you His own in Baptism, cares for you. Jesus Christ knows your pain and provides the Word and Sacraments to sustain you in this life. The Holy Spirit grants you faith and sends faithful Christian brothers and sisters to care for you in the good times and the bad. Mental illness is a reminder that we are sinful and broken. Let your identity as a redeemed child of God remind you that nothing on earth or in heaven can separate you from the love of God through Christ Jesus, your Lord.

# On Hurt

*Sarah Gulseth*

"The Lord is my strength and my song, And He has become my salvation." Psalm 118:14

Dear sister in Christ,

How are you underneath the "Good, how are you?" Do you feel hurt, worn down by the consequences of this broken world? Scoot over a bit, and let me sit with you to lift your burden from your shoulders for a little while. (We might even sing a hymn.)

Maybe you've been languishing in the valley of sorrow for longer than you can remember. Maybe the devil's arrows have hit their marks a little too frequently. Maybe you're reeling from a sudden gut-wrenching turn of events. Maybe life's little irritations and inconveniences have built to a breaking point. Or maybe the heavy sighs have become your normal, and your nervous system can't remember what it feels like to breathe easily.

I see you. I've been there, too. So has the Psalmist: "I am weary with my moaning;

every night I flood my bed with tears; I drench my couch with my weeping. My eye wastes away because of grief; it grows weak because of all my foes." (Psalm 6:6-7)

Sometimes, the only thing we can do is cry out to the Lord for mercy—that guttural scream emanating from depths you didn't know u had. And while I can only imagine the sound of your cries for mercy, and I can't fix it for you, I can give you hope. Let me wrap your soul in the promises of Jesus with the words on this page.

So, breathe deeply, relax your shoulders, and unclench your jaw. You are not alone, and you are deeply loved. Jesus is with you, and I'm going to tell you how (even if you already know).

It's easy to feel alone when the burdens we bear are on the inside when no one can see the swirl of emotions in our heads. It's easy to pull the covers tight and not want anyone to see the cuts and bruises on our hearts. And while you may feel alone, you are not. Jesus sees you. I see you.

I know what it is to lament, to have those words, "How long, O Lord?" burned in your throat, like they were for David in Psalm 13. What happens when it feels like God isn't listening, when things keep going wrong, day after day, and the weariness settles in your bones?

> "I say to God, my rock: 'Why have you forgotten me? Why do I go mourning because of the oppression of the enemy?' As with a deadly wound in my bones, my adversaries taunt me, while they say to me all the day long, 'Where is your God?'" (Psalm 42:9-10)

Here's the thing, dear sister. The devil wants you to despair. He wants you to think God doesn't care, that you're better off alone, that Jesus does not save you. That just because we can only hear silence, God must be ignoring us. But you and I both know that the devil is spewing lies to your face. In our own time-bound lives, God can feel distant when things are hard, and our hearts are hurting. But you know the truth, that He promises to be with you. He knows your every thought, every emotion, every bit of physical pain. He promises to hear our prayers, and He answers every one of them in His own time and His own way. These verses from Psalm 42 are my absolute favorite when my soul is tempted to despair: "Why are you cast down, O my soul, and why are you in turmoil within me? Hope in God; for I shall again praise him, my salvation and my God." (Psalm 42:11)

When I hurt, I want to know "why." We're logical beings and would really love an answer for why God allows us to suffer in these ways. I won't lie to you; I don't have the answer for your pain or mine. We might not know the answer on this side of the resurrection, and that can be hard to live with. What I do know, though, is that God draws us near to Him in these times of distress. "My grace is sufficient for you, for my power is made perfect in weakness" (2 Corinthians 12:9). When we allow ourselves to be enveloped by Jesus' love amid suffering, He gives us the strength to process our big emotions, to take the next step forward, to have the hard conversation.

But sometimes, the world seems to pile on new suffering and pain in a cruel layer cake, not caring that we haven't digested yesterday's grief just yet. One problem after another piles up, and it feels like the devil is having target practice on your soul. When we have those "groanings too deep for words" (Romans 8:26b), we cry to the Lord who promises to hear us. But these aren't just empty complaints because Christ knows your heart. We can cry out to God because we know that He loves us with a steadfast love beyond our comprehension. Our pain and hurt may not end until the resurrection. Come soon, Lord Jesus! But while we wait, we have comfort that only Christ can give us in His Word and Sacraments. He promises to be in those Gifts for us, and His promises are true.

It's the beautiful twist, dear sister, the thing that turns the world on its head. The thing that sends the devil packing: When we lament, Christ hears us, and He is with us. Christ will bear you through the evil days with more steadfast love than we can even imagine.

If thou but trust in God to guide thee And hope in Him through all thy ways, He'll give thee strength, whate'er betide thee, And bear thee through the evil days. Who trusts in God's unchanging love Builds on the rock that naught can move. (Lutheran Service Book 750, st. 1)

It feels unfair to suffer, to be hurt by others, to be hurt by our own faults and failures. We suffer the consequences of sin in this world. But we have a God of reconciliation and redemption. He promises redemption to the contrite spirit. In the midst of our pain, we cry to the Lord, and He hears us. And while we may still suffer the consequences of sin, our ultimate rest is in Jesus and His promise of a redeemed New Creation.

"But I have trusted in your steadfast love; my heart shall rejoice in your salvation. I will sing to the Lord, because he has dealt bountifully with me." (Psalm 13:5-6)

You have a weapon against the lies of the devil and the world that is more powerful than anything: the Words of Christ. Those words were etched on your heart when you received the Spirit in Baptism. Nothing, absolutely nothing, can take that away from you. When the devil tries to make you doubt that Christ knows you and loves you, you can call him a liar because you have the promises of Christ. You can sing the words of our hymnody that confess what is true: the devil is defeated, and Christ has won the victory for us!

The foe in triumph shouted When Christ lay in the tomb; But lo, he now is routed, His boast is turned to gloom. For Christ again is free; In glorious victory He who is strong to save Has triumphed o'er the grave. (Lutheran Service Book 467, st. 2)

Sometimes, I think about that Good Friday when the devil believed he had won. Can you imagine his surprise when Christ descended to Hell and declared victory over the grave? And that victory is YOUR victory! Jesus took all of your sin, your pain, your shame, into His body and redeemed all of them in His resurrected flesh. Christ is risen! He is risen indeed, alleluia! Death is swallowed up by death; you were buried by Baptism into Christ's death. But just as He was raised, you, too, will rise again and live in Him! The devil hates to hear you confess it, but you, dear sister, are a child of God, and Satan cannot touch you!

Satan, I defy thee; Death, I now decry thee; Fear, I bid thee cease. World, thou shalt not harm me Nor thy threats alarm me While I sing of peace. God's great pow'r Guards ev'ry hour; Earth and all its depths adore Him, Silent bow before Him. (Lutheran Service Book 743, st. 3)

Singing reaches into the depths of our souls with God's promises to us. And when you sing out loud, you're confessing to yourself into your own ears what you know to be true in your heart. When you're hurt, when you feel the pain of this world, when the devil tries to sow seeds of despair, sing all the more boldly! This is your battle cry against the wiles of the devil, as James says (4:7), "Resist the devil, and he will flee from you."

We have the ultimate hope in the promise of the resurrection. "On the last day, He will raise me and all the dead, and bring eternal life to me and all believers in Christ. This is most certainly true" (Luther's Small Catechism). Christ will draw you to His side in the resurrection, and we will live with Him forever. "He will wipe away every tear from their eyes, and death shall be no more, neither shall there be mourning, nor crying, nor pain anymore, for the former things have passed away." (Revelation 21:4)

So, dear sister, I can't fix your pain, your hurt, your grief. But Jesus can and does. Cling to your Baptism. Cling to the cross and Christ's promises of forgiveness, life, and salvation we receive through His sacraments.

Pray with me:

In suff'ring be Thy love my peace, In weakness be Thy love my pow'r; And when the storms of life shall cease, O Jesus, in that final hour, Be Thou my rod and staff and guide, And draw me safely to Thy side! (Lutheran Service Book 683, st. 4)

Christ be with you, dear sister.

# On Loss

*Lisa Goodman*

Truth: At some point, you will experience loss. It might be something small that you cope with, or it might be something bigger that's harder to move on from. You have probably already experienced a small loss, and maybe you have already experienced that bigger loss, even at your young age. Loss looks different depending on who you talk to. It could be simple—losing a physical item or sitting on the bench due to an injury. Maybe it's something bigger, though—the death of a loved one, parents divorcing, or the end of a friendship you cherished. Sometimes, we can even bring loss on ourselves. Under the guise of self-preservation, we might think that we are pushing people away because we believe we aren't worth their love, but the reality is that doubt and worry have caused another lost relationship. The common thread that loss has, no matter what it looks like, is that it hurts. Truth: Sin breaks stuff—and that hurts.

Growing up is hard at all stages, and I'm sorry for what you have been through. When you are a child, you experience loss that seems easier to move on from. As you get older, it hits harder and becomes more difficult. This may even be true of those losses you experienced when you were younger that seemed easy then, but now you may realize were not so easy. You better understand the consequences of what you have lost. Here is another hard truth: Loss, especially big loss (whatever that looks like), never goes away. While the marks of it ıt heal as you move away from it, you will feel the consequences at times you least expect. Loss and the consequences we feel from it are because of sin in the world. We can't avoid sin, and so, unfortunately, we can't avoid loss and the pain that comes from it.

Sweet sister in Christ, I have been there, and I have felt that pain of loss. Do you know who else has been there? Jesus Christ Himself. We know that He felt loss and grief because we hear about it in John 11. When His friend, Lazarus, died, Scripture tells us that "Jesus wept" when this happened. He was clearly affected by this loss.

The question is, where do we go from here? I don't know what you have experienced, but I'm guessing you don't need to hear "Keep your chin up!" or "You're strong; you'll get through this!" or "There is a reason for everything." You might not feel strong right now, and you may never know the reason, so these sentiments are not helpful. What I will do is give you permission to grieve and have moments where you are not strong. To mourn. If God is allowed to do it, so are you. I recently came across the idea that grief is not the enemy of faith. You do not have less faith because you are feeling this loss, and it is okay to miss what you have lost. And another thing—it is still ok to mourn that lost scholarship, that lost relationship, that lost person ten, twenty, even fifty years down the road.

Here is the caveat to this. We do have hope, even in loss. In 1 Thessalonians 4, Paul tells us that because of the death and resurrection of Jesus Christ, we can grieve with hope. In this passage, Paul is referencing grieving our brothers and sisters who have fallen asleep in Christ, but this grief, this mourning, this loss we experience—it is informed not by the world but by the Gospel. This may feel contradictory. Experience your loss, but be happy while you do it? No, loss of any nature is not a happy thing. Hope and happiness are not the same things.

In the most basic sense of the word, hope is a sense of trust in something. Our trust, our hope, lies in Jesus Christ. When you are going through it, this is really hard to see. Loss can lead to a very dark place, and it can be hard to see hope there. Sometimes, you may need another person, or people, to see it for you. Who are your people? Who is your tribe? Truth: You cannot get through this on your own. As humans, we were not created to be alone. We have a religion where we rely on that which is outside of us. God saw from the start that it was not good for us to be on our own. This is why he created Eve for Adam.

He gives you people, too. He puts people in our lives and works through them, just like Paul talks about in Philippians 4. Paul thanks the people of Phillipi for helping carry his needs and his burdens. Think again of the people in your life. Who are the people who can help you see hope when you are having a hard time seeing it yourself? Maybe you can turn to your parents, your pastor, or your best friend. Don't be afraid of letting them know how deeply your loss has affected you. It's ok to cry. It's ok to despair and wallow and shout, "God, why did this happen?" All of this is normal in grief. David did this exact thing in the Psalms of Lament. In these Psalms where he cries out, there is always a "but" or a "yet' that firmly roots him in God's promises. Just because you are asking "why?" doesn't mean you are rejecting God. Anger comes with loss, and it's ok to be angry. Your friends will help you through these feelings. Your God will help you through your misery because he does not abandon you. Through these trials, he has given you hope. Even if you are having trouble feeling this hope—this trust in something outside of you—for yourself, these people will give you the reminder and speak the words out loud that Jesus Christ lived and died for you. Because of this, while this loss may hurt and may stay with you through this life, you have something greater to look to. You have your own resurrection through Christ. You have forgiveness through Christ (and so do the others in whatever you are going through).

Along with these things, this is a reminder to you that you have people. You have a community that loves you and wants to be with you and help carry you through the fear and sorrow you are feeling right now. This community can bring Jesus to you and you to Communion with Jesus. At the rail, we get to eat and drink Jesus' Body and Blood in Holy Communion with our brothers and sisters in Christ. We get to receive peace and begin healing from our loss through our Savior, who knows exactly what you are feeling.

Allow yourself to feel these things but try not to stay there for too long. Take a walk, play a game, make dinner. These small actions might not seem like much, but finding a place to put your energy and redirect your mind can give you clarity that may be hard to feel lately. Do these things with other people. Find your community and let them remind you of the hope Jesus gives.

Most of all, lean on your Baptism. Here, you find assurance that Christ has not and will not leave you. He died for you; this is how precious you are to Him. And when you despair because of the sin that causes loss in your life, lean on your community so that they might help remind you that you are not alone. Not only do you have them, but you have Christ, who is with you now and even ten, twenty, or fifty years down the road. Loss hurts, and it can be different for everyone. Thanks be to God that we have a community to work through our losses and point us to Christ. Take heart; He has overcome the world.

# On Life

*Michelle Bauman*

Dear Sister in Christ,

Life. It's the topic I've been assigned to write to you about, and I'll be honest; it's a little daunting. Not the writing, per se, but the topic itself because there's simply so MUCH to say.

So, I've been contemplating… I've been asking myself, "What does she need to know? How can I best prepare her for what's to come? What does she need to hear me say?

What is the commonality in all of these questions?" YOU. And YOU are exactly where I want to begin.

So, let's start with the basics. Let's begin with identity. Who are you anyway?

You are, fundamentally, a human being, and according to dictionary.com, a human being is "any individual of the genus Homo, especially a member of the species Homo sapiens." In other words, you are part of a category of creatures. Different from other creatures, you have, proportionally, a larger brain, and you use that massive brain to make art, create language, strategize and problem solve, and display, among many other emotions, love, and empathy. This scientific categorization also means that your body is designed to walk on two legs rather than four, and at the end of your arms, you have hands with opposable thumbs that enable you to grasp pencils and swing hammers with both power and precision.

And, as long as you can swing a hammer with power and precision, this definition is not only true but observable. It's scientifically accurate. But, let's be honest, it's also woefully incomplete.

Why? Because you are much more than a member of a species. The Scriptures testify to this truth again and again, and this testimony begins at the beginning. Genesis 1 and 2 not only describe the preparatory work God carried out for human beings—His creation of a perfect, life-sustaining garden in a world full of wonders—but the text also describes His intimate work to hand form the pinnacle of His creation: humanity.

Genesis 1:26 says, "Then God said, 'Let us make man in our image, after our likeness. And let them have dominion over the fish of the sea and over the birds of the heavens and over the livestock and over all the earth and over every creeping thing that creeps on the earth." Humans were made in the image of God. Broken by sin, our image is restored in Christ.

Why is that important? Because you were made for life. From the moment God formed you in your mother's womb, you were made for eternity; yes, you were made to live FOREVER. Now, that doesn't mean you'll never die. Unless Jesus comes again, you'll have to pass through that valley, too. But it does mean that God will not forsake you. It means He plans to walk with you through this veil of tears and bring you into the glory that awaits. It also means that despite your brokenness and hardships and sin, you have HOPE, and that hope is sure and certain because it depends on Christ.

Yes, your life has inherent value, and that value does not reside in your beauty or your brains. It has no connection to your athletic or artistic abilities; it's not tied to your height or weight or any of your physical features. True, these gifts are wonderful, and they can certainly be used in service to others, but your value and worth are not tied to them. Your value, your worth, is tied to God.

How has God made you valuable? Let me count the ways....

First, your life is valuable because it was handmade by God Himself. Psalm 139 attests to this fact, "For you formed my inward parts; you knitted me together in my mother's womb. I praise you, for I am fearfully and wonderfully made" (Psalm 139:13-14). Not only did God form you, a unique and irreplaceable human being, but He also wrote your name in His Book of Life.

And you know what's even more amazing? He had you in mind even before the beginning of time itself. Ephesians 1:3-4 states, "Blessed be the God and Father of our Lord Jesus Christ, who has blessed us in Christ with every spiritual blessing in the heavenly places, even as he chose us in him **before the foundation of the world**, that we should be holy and blameless before him." (emphasis mine)

Second, you were not only created by God Himself but you have also been redeemed. Galatians 4:4-5 reminds us that "when the fullness of time had come, God sent forth his Son, born of woman, born under the law, to redeem those who were under the law, so that we might receive adoption as sons." You, daughter of the most high King, have received the inheritance of the firstborn Son, Christ. Bought back by His holy sacrifice, you have become an heir of eternal life. As both a child of God and heir to heaven, your life has inherent value.

How did you become the heir of God Himself? Through your Baptism. This is yet another reason your life is valuable. In water combined with God's Holy Word, you were called to faith. Your sinful flesh died, and you were brought back to life in Christ. Through this first death and resurrection, your body was made a temple of the Holy Spirit. You are a beloved child of God, one in whom the Holy Spirit dwells.

Yes, by God's Gift and God's grace, you have been created, redeemed, and called. Because of God's Work, your life has inherent value and meaning.

Now that we've established your worth, let's talk about the worth and value of others. You see, the truth is, life doesn't exist apart from the God who is LIFE. It cannot. God is both the author and sustainer of life. He determines when and where life comes to be, and life is always intended to be a gift. That means there are no unplanned pregnancies. There are no unloved or unwanted children. And there are no accidents. God plans, loves, and desires every life He has created to be with Him for all eternity.

And what is true of babies in the womb is also true of the child diagnosed with a disability. It's true of the teen suffering from loneliness and depression and the young woman engaged in self-harm. It's just as true of the veteran with PTSD and suicidal ideation as it is of the individual diagnosed with terminal cancer, the mother and father mourning the loss of their stillborn child, or the young man and woman addicted to pornography. Every life is valuable: the Muslim and the atheist, the immigrant and the homeless, the trafficked and the trafficker.

And you.

God loves every human being despite our sin and brokenness. Even more, He enters into that brokenness with us, wading through the muck of sin, taking it onto Himself so that we might be made new. Christ's holy and innocent blood washes us clean in our baptismal waters and makes us whole. Galatians 3:13 reminds us that "Christ redeemed us from the curse of the law by becoming the curse for us." He exchanged our clothes for His and made us heirs of the Gifts of heaven.

His work in our lives not only shapes how we view ourselves (as beloved children of God) but also how we see the lives of others (as gifts to us and to the world). His work in our lives enables us to reach out in service toward those in need, even when they are less than desirable and even when they are covered in the sludge of sin. Because Christ carries our cross, we can help others carry theirs.

How does this happen? Through our vocations. God not only places us in relationships but also works through those relationships, those vocations, to uphold our lives and enable us to uphold the lives of others.

And by God's grace, we do! God's life-affirming love is felt through donations: diapers to pregnancy care centers and hygiene kits to homeless shelters. It's heard when we encourage the depressed and educate communities on human trafficking. It's revealed through aid to refugees, food collections for the impoverished, and Christmas gifts to families in need.

God's life-affirming work also happens in small things, in daily acts of service like making dinner for your family, running errands for Mom, and taking out the trash for Dad. You reveal Christ when you bandage a child's knee, visit a shut-in, and put the best construction on the actions of others. Whether you know it or not, you help others bear their crosses daily, and in so doing, you uphold their lives.

Life work. It looks a lot like CHRIST IN YOU. It is the good work that overflows onto others because your cup is so full of His goodness that you are moved to share mercy with your neighbors. Why? Because their lives are valuable, too.

And that brings us back to the beginning, doesn't it? Who are you? You are Christian. You are a beloved child of God. Created, redeemed, and called, you are inherently valuable because of God's work in your life. And because He is in you, you have become a light to the world.

May you rejoice in the life God has given you, dear Sister in Christ. May you find much joy and purpose as you uphold the lives of others, and may you shine brightly for HIM!

In Christ 4 Life,
Michelle Bauman

# On Expectations

*Paige Rebber*

Are you good enough? When you're lying in bed at night thinking about all of the things that you did during the day, how do you measure up? Did you do and say all that was expected of you? What if you didn't?

So many things are expected of us. We set the bar so high that the only way to reach it is to be perfect. So that's what we do. We try to be the perfect wife, the perfect daughter, the perfect friend, the perfect Christian. We expect ourselves to act in a certain way, say certain things, don't do this, always do that, be better, and it's overwhelming. Then, the expectations of the world pile on top of the expectations we have of ourselves. Be more tolerant of things, wear this, don't wear that, look pretty, but don't try too hard. It seems everywhere you turn, there is a standard to fulfill. There are even expectations quoted to us based in Scripture: "Wives, submit to your husbands (Ephesians 5:22)," "be a Proverbs 31 woman," "cover your head and submit to the proper authorities (1 Corinthians 11:2-16)," "be respectable, modest, and learn in all submissiveness (1 Timothy 2:9-15)," "keep silent in church (1 Corinthians 14:34-35)." It seems that this is what is expected of women, and it's a heavy burden. After all, if this is truly what a woman is expected to be and expected to do, what happens when I fail to do so? What if I can't live up to being a Proverbs 31 woman? What if I don't live out what Paul says is right of a woman in the church? Am I a terrible woman in the eyes of the Lord if I don't consistently do these things? Can we challenge the expectations that Christians place on women without challenging the Scriptures themselves? What about other Christians' expectations? Especially men? How do I look to them? What if? What if? What if?

We get so wrapped up in trying to be this perfect woman. These expectations weigh us down. Then, to make matters worse, everyone's definition of what it means to be perfect is different, so the expectations get tangled up and weigh us down even more. This whole mess is self-destructive. How do we view ourselves when we know we can't fulfill God's expectations? We try to reach that bar over and over again, yet it always escapes our grasp. Nevertheless, we push on, saying that maybe this time will be different, still trying our hardest with all our strength to reach that bar that will make us good enough. There is so much emphasis on being good enough, but what is "good enough?" God's Law sets a perfect standard we know of which we fall short. What about the world's false expectations? What about misunderstandings or misappropriations of Scripture that are imposed on Christians? These are not the law but are treated like the Law. You see, by trying to set these high perfectionistic expectations for ourselves, we live in fear of the inevitable day that we are seen as not living up to all these expectations. That's terrifying. The bar is so incredibly high that we have made it utterly unattainable in our pursuit of perceived perfection by meeting every expectation.

No matter how much we think we can do all of this and reach perfection on our own, we have to realize that we are not perfect. The only thing we can consistently expect of ourselves is that we will mess up. That's what it's like to live in sin. It's messy; it's uncomfortable; and it's damning. That's why we have to remember who the Perfect One actually is and how we relate to Him. All of the expectations laid out for us are relational. This relationship is based on our Baptism and Him in whom we are baptized. Go back and look at these expectations in Scripture through the lens of who you really are: a baptized child of Christ. His expectation for us is that we love the Lord our God with all our heart, soul, and mind and love our neighbor as ourselves—a goal that is unattainable outside of grace, which is given to us freely through Christ. Grace is the filter through which all of our expectations run.

When we look at the expectations laid out in Scripture, they seem like unattainable goals, especially if you view them as a laundry list of things you need to check off before any expectations can actually be met. In our sinful condition, we are not capable of judging what is good, but we try. I certainly don't make linen garments and sell them, so I've already failed in one of the tasks laid out in Proverbs 31. But is this a law? I don't cover my head in church, so that must mean that I'm not submitting correctly and have failed 1 Corinthians 11. But what does this mean? I'm going into a church work vocation; does that mean I have ignored 1 Timothy 2 and 1 Corinthians 14? It is easy to make all these passages law-heavy, read them at face value, and take them out of context. The context that is key for all of these passages is the relational aspect between us and Christ. How does the Proverbs 31 woman relate to Christ? What is expected of her? She fears Him as she goes about her daily tasks, and He clothes her with dignity and righteousness. She doesn't have to complete the checklists of tasks to earn that dignity and righteousness. It is freely given through the death and resurrection of the One who watches over and protects her.

What about the woman who doesn't cover her head in church? Whether or not you veil (a choice that is yours in Christian freedom), the real issue is submission and headship. A Christian woman is an image of the church, and the church submits to Christ. This image draws on the relationship Paul lays out in Ephesians 5 regarding husbands and wives. This relationship, understood through Christ and the church, is defined by love, not power. Wives should not dishonor their husbands, but is that conveyed today through head coverings or something else? So whether or not you veil, in love, you still fulfill the expectation of submission to Christ as the head of the church. What about the woman who is pursuing a church work vocation such as a Deaconess? You are in no way ignoring the Scripture when you choose to work in Christ's church. It is not an attempt to usurp the office of the ministry but rather to support it. Women should not speak in church—that's true, as we don't preach. However, we are able to offer encouragement through the words of Scripture and in acts of mercy, as every Christian is called to do. Women facilitate the bonds of fellowship in the church as well as outside the church in the roles unique to them. The expectation is that she learns from the pastor and submits to him as she carries out her role in service to Christ, and that is a blessing.

All of these things are expectations of Law, but they are given to us in the freedom of the Gospel. We are only free in the Gospel if the Law is already fulfilled somewhere. The expectation to be perfect demanded in the Law is fulfilled in Christ already. So just try. You are free to fail. You are free to not "be enough" because Christ is enough for you. He has fulfilled the expectations you're being measured against. You don't have to. There is grace for you. Under the Gospel, these things are a joy to do, not a burden. The expectation is fulfilled in Christ. Just try.

We are sinners and will fall short, but that doesn't mean that our efforts are in vain. Lean on your Baptism. Lean on Christ. The whole point of these expectations is not to defeat you but to lift you up and give you a place. These aren't rules to follow because we are somehow less than and have to work harder to earn the grace that Christ gives. Our work can't do anything; grace is a Gift. It's a Gift we have even if we fail to meet the expectations that we have of ourselves. It is a Gift given to us not by our own works but by the work of Christ and Him alone. There is no expectation we can fulfill in the eyes of God on our own. If we could, there would be no need for Christ.

What about the expectations of society? It is so tempting to look in the mirror and see only our flaws: too fat, no muscle, not pretty, beat down, ugly, worn out, not enough. Society expects perfection in the mirror, but buried in our sinful condition, we can't see that. The reality is that we are sinners who desperately need someone who can fulfill all of the expectations of the Law. This person is Christ. He is the one who was born for you, baptized for you, suffered, bled, and died for you. He is the one who shouldered all of the expectations of the world and cried, "It is finished!" Then He rose, laying all of the expectations of the Law that condemned us in the grave. We are now clothed in righteousness. All expectations have been fulfilled for us. When you look in the mirror, see His perfection covering you because you are baptized. You are His. You are enough because He is more than enough for you.

Will we ever be good enough on our own? No. Thanks be to God that through our Baptism, we are free from all of those things that threaten to overwhelm us. Expectations are good, but only as they are measured by grace. Satan can use expectations to turn us away from Christ and into ourselves, giving us the false hope that we could ever reach that standard of perfection. It skews our identity to be self-reliant. However, our identity is not in ourselves and what we can do. Our identity is in Christ. We are not defined by what we can do but by what has been done for us. Perfection isn't a goal you have to reach, but it is what you have and what you are because of Jesus! You are made new; you and your expectations are yoked to Christ, who carries your burdens and fulfills all righteousness for you. So go, live in the peace and comfort that Christ has won for you in His death and resurrection. Breathe.

www.ingramcontent.com/pod-product-compliance
Lightning Source LLC
Chambersburg PA
CBHW020415130626
46549CB00006B/2567